YOUR BABY'S MIND

How to Make the Most of the Critical First Two Years

S. H. Jacob, Ph.D.

AuthorHouse™
1663 Liberty Drive, Suite 200
Bloomington, IN 47403
www.authorhouse.com
Phone: 1-800-839-8640

First published by AuthorHouse 03/09/2009

ISBN:1- 9781-4343-6936-9

This publication is designed to provide accurate information with regard to the subject matter covered. It is not, and is not intended to, be a substitute for consultation with a qualified physician or therapist. If medical advice or other expert assistance is required, the services of a competent professional in the field should by sought.

Printed in the United States of America
Bloomington, Indiana

This book is printed on acid-free paper.

To my wife Diana and our
twin boys, Koby and Jeremy.

I would like to thank Stephanie Jeong with selecting the images contained in this book and creating such an outstanding, user-friendly design.

contents

before you begin

Welcome to *Your Baby's Mind: How to Make the
Most of the Critical First Two Years.* Like many conscien-
tious parents, you may feel that it is never too early to give
your baby a good start in life. You are absolutely correct.
We have known for a few decades now that a child's first
two years of life are the most important in his intellectual
development. Today, we know even more. Not only are the
first two years the most important in your child's cognitive
development; they also set the stage for everything to follow.

In short, these years are the foundation for your child's future learning and development. The approach you take and the activities you focus on with your child will have a profound influence on his future development.

So how do you begin? You may be confused by the many different products and programs that claim to produce infant geniuses; you may even be skeptical. You are right to be so. Your baby thrives on activities that nurture the natural processes of his mind, not ones that produce superficially impressive results. Problem solving, creativity, means-ends, causality, object concept, space relations—these are the stuff from which thoughtful intelligence is made. My comprehensive developmental approach is the antidote for meaningless learning, empty verbalisms, flash cards, and rote memorization. Instead of training your baby to produce predetermined responses, you will engage in activities geared to the way your baby adapts, learns, discovers, and invents—the way he naturally uses his intelligence. Instead of teaching him a repertoire of tricks, you will be helping your baby build a powerful foundation for future learning, and instilling a lifelong love of learning, discovery, and invention.

Knowledge is the best tool that you as a parent have, and I am privileged to share with you what I have learned in the over three decades I have researched, taught, and written about cognitive development. I base my approach on the most widely accepted theory of cognitive development to date—that of Jean Piaget, the world-renowned psychologist under whom I had the honor of studying twenty-five years ago. As we explore the profound changes your child undergoes in the first two years of life, you will come to see—as I have—that babies are born active knowledge-seeking, knowledge-making, know-how-inventing beings.

Babies the world over develop in discrete, well-known stages. Knowing how your baby makes meaning of his experiences at each of these stages will provide you with a road map to guide your baby's intellectual development, enhancing and enriching the process by engaging him in meaningful, stage-appropriate activities.

In addition to describing the abilities your baby has at each stage of development and how psychologists have reached their conclusions about the critical importance of the first two years, I will provide you with numerous illustrated games, activities, and interactions you can use to engage, enhance, and transform your baby's mind. Your baby will not only derive beneficial long-term results from these activities, but he will also have fun! I want you to be in charge of this process, so I provide you with both the research behind my approach and concrete suggestions for employing it to enable you to be creative in this wonderfully rewarding journey. Understanding what you're doing and why will allow you to create your own enriching experiences.

I want to give you the tools and the confidence you need to enable your baby to reach his full intellectual potential. Your baby's mind is perhaps the most miraculous thing you will ever encounter—and the more you know, the more miraculous the encounter becomes. Enjoy this most enlightening and joyful time of your life!

Dr. S. H. Jacob
Temecula, California

what is the mind?

What is this mystery we call "mind?" For centuries philosophers and psychologists have debated this question without a definitive answer. Some say that the mind is nothing more than the brain's electrochemical activity. Others, including me, believe the mind is not purely the physical organ we know as the brain, but rather that it is a process of making meaning out of the interactions with things and people that we encounter every day.

Most professionals would agree that the mind is the product of three types of knowing: (1) knowledge (what something is, like what a rattle is); (2) know-how (how to do something, like how to shake the rattle to make noise); and (3) a fixed body of information (the word "rattle," or that a green traffic signal means "go.") These components of the mind develop together as your baby grows, expanding as her experience of the world around her increases.

When it comes to "intelligence," psychologists fall into two camps. Some think of intelligence as something that can be measured. These psychologists rely on a test that compares your child's performance to that of other children her own age. They generally call this an IQ test (a test of one's intelligence quotient). IQ, of course, is a score, a number that implies some finality. For babies, this score has been referred to as a developmental quotient, or a DQ.

The alternative way to look at intelligence, the one advanced in this book, is to view it as a process that cannot—and should not—be assigned a number precisely because it has no finality. In this view, human action defines intelligence. Thus, intelligence is the ability to relate experiences to what a person already knows and to invent new schemes for knowing something. It is the ability to manipulate, transform, play with, and abstract meaning from our interactions with objects, events, and people. In this approach, one would describe what a child can do rather than attempt to ascribe a score to her abilities.

To use a metaphor, intelligence is not a station you arrive at; rather, it is a manner of traveling. Intelligence represents ways of knowing, ways of making meaning. Meaning making is the only natural work of intelligence. Intelligence is not only what your child has memorized; it is not only whether she can recite the alphabet or count from one to ten, or name some of the colors. These are important ingredients of the intellectual process, but by themselves, they do not constitute intelligence. Intelligence, in large part, refers to ways of manipulating these ingredients.

The moment your baby is born, she already knows something—she knows how to hear, see, smell, feel, and taste. In fact, before she is born, she can distinguish her mother's voice from someone else's, and she can even distinguish her own mother's language from another language! Your baby also knows how to react to different stimuli through her reflexes, like grasping with her hands when you touch the palms of her hand. Your baby quickly builds on these sensory and motor beginnings by linking them with one another in more and more elaborate ways, resulting in more diverse repertoires of actions.

As your child grows older, her manipulations become more internalized, meaning she will be able to carry them out in her head. In the first six months of life, you can expect your child's intellectual development to be restricted to her sensory (seeing, hearing, feeling, tasting, smelling) and motor (such as grasping or mouthing) functions. But in the second half of her first year she'll begin to mentally represent things; in other words, she'll be able to see them in her mind's eye.

For example, she'll be able to know that you are somewhere in the house even though she can't see you. Yet at that age, six months, she will still struggle with other intellectual tasks. The following simple problem, for example, will be beyond her abilities: She will likely struggle to retrieve a toy through the slats of a crib, only to give up and cry because the toy simply won't slip through the slats in its current position. But around the time she turns ten months, she will grab the toy and turn it so it is parallel to the slats, thereby easily slipping it through.

From the very beginning, your baby's mind is naturally motivated to make meaning of her encounters. It does so in three ways: First, by interacting with people and objects your baby will discover features of the objects, such as what color they are, what they feel like, what sounds they make, what they taste like, and so on. In this way, she will be forming her own rudimentary knowledge of science. Second, by interacting with people and objects, she will invent a repertoire of know-how, such as how to grasp a toy, how to rotate it, how to mouth it, how to transfer it from one hand to another, or how to pull and push it. In the first two years or so, this inventive process leads to a form of logic—the logic of actions. For example, by the time your baby is ten months old, she'll be able to bring a toy within her reach by pulling on the blanket that it rests on! This beautiful little example of intelligence at work neatly illustrates how your baby invents a solution to accomplish her goal. Thirdly, by interacting with people and objects, she will accumulate conventional knowledge; that is, she will learn things having to do with her culture, such as language, songs, rhymes, and rituals.

In short, intelligence encompasses many areas of knowledge. It is more than just a score on a test, no matter how carefully constructed the test may be. So what do we mean when we say that someone is intelligent? First, we mean he is able to know in increasingly more abstract ways; even if objects are far away from him in space or time, such as an astronomer who studies distant stars, or a chess master who plans a strategy to anticipate an opponent's moves. Second, we mean he is intellectually flexible, able to find many solutions to a given problem. If this chess move doesn't work, then this other one may. Finally, we mean he is quicker at the task—he is able to rapidly assimilate encounters into his previous knowledge or create an understanding of new experiences.

And so it is with your baby. As your child grows older, she will be able to know in more and more abstract ways, creatively solve problems to find different paths to the same end, and perform tasks rapidly. This is how she forms her "mind." So you have a lot to look forward to!

As a parent, you naturally want to nurture your baby's intellectual development. In the next two chapters we will explore what psychologists know about early intellectual development, and how you can use this knowledge not only to support your baby's own creativity and curiosity, but also to critically evaluate the claims made by many educational toys and methods popular today. What I advocate is not a gimmick or product, but an educational psychology based on extensive scientific research, one that will allow your child to reach her fullest potential through her own efforts, guided and supported by you.

2

making meaning: that's what it's all about

Active Enrichment

My first task is to show you exactly how your baby is a meaning maker; and secondly, to help you understand-stage by stage-what your baby can do and how you can become an even better coach during each stage. Understanding your baby's intellectual development will not only be greatly rewarding for you, but it will help you produce highly enriching experiences for your baby.

The following points form the core of my approach:

BABIES ARE KNOWLEDGE MAKERS.

Babies learn best by using their senses and manipulating things in order to learn about them. They make meaning of things by perceiving and acting on them. Their innate curiosity drives them to explore and invent. They are also innately equipped to learn any human language they encounter.

MEANING LIES IN INDIVIDUALS, NOT IN OBJECTS.

People determine the meaning of an object, a process, or a concept, and this meaning may be different from one individual to the next. A person's understanding of an object, a concept, or a principle depends on his present ways of knowing and what he already knows about it.

KNOWLEDGE IS ITS OWN REWARD.

Understanding, solving problems, being creative, and making meaning do not depend on outside rewards for motivation–they have their own inherent rewards.

MEANING IS PERSONAL AND PLURALISTIC.

Learning is a supremely personal, constructive process. The best way to learn something is to relate it to what you already know. Your baby learns the same way. Start with what your child already knows and can do. Babies learn best when they are given a chance to manipulate, transform, and create knowledge for themselves.

TO KNOW IS TO ACT.

The process of doing something is more important than simply getting the right result. The emphasis should be on learning how to learn, how to think—not merely learning specific responses to certain cues.

WE BUILD INTELLIGENCE BY EMPHASIZING THE WAYS OF KNOWING.

Nurturing the underlying processes of intelligence requires promoting an attitude that permits babies and young children to be physically and mentally active, to discover through their spontaneous actions, and to invent as necessary. In doing so, we respect—and conform to—the natural, spontaneous ways children form knowledge.

THE STAGES OF DEVELOPMENT DEFINE THE LIMITS OF THE KNOWLEDGE MAKING PROCESS.

Matching your baby's stage of development with appropriately chosen toys, materials, and activities is extremely important. Without this proper match, your child might be frustrated or bored.

SOCIAL CONTEXT IS THE KEY TO HEALTHY COGNITIVE DEVELOPMENT.

Finally, we must remember that all intellectual development occurs in an appropriate social context. Babies develop their fullest potential through exploration and play, with great latitude to choose what they are interested in, especially in an atmosphere of unconditional love, encouragement, support, and coaching. The support and guidance that you provide quite naturally is crucial to your baby's intellectual development. For example, you, like most parents, will show your toddler how to fit an object into the right slot in a shape sorter. And you will do this time and time again—tirelessly—until he does it on his own. You will pick a task that your baby can't quite do by himself and coach him to do it, spurring his development forward. Then as your baby's competence increases, you'll step back, allowing him more and more freedom to accomplish the task on his own.

By seizing upon and developing the very natural tendencies of our babies to inquire, discover, test, evaluate, search, and invent, our society can advance itself. It is not sufficient to transmit our culture's ready-made knowledge to our children. We must understand their inherent creative tendencies and nurture them. Ultimately, we want to enable our babies to become independent thinkers, discovers, and inventors.

To provide children with this support from the early days of infancy onward is in keeping with developmental psychology's most fundamental principles. The enrichment approach I recommend in this book contains all the elements of a return to sound child-rearing concepts arranged to work in complete harmony with the ways babies develop. This approach involves nurturing and educating our children's underlying processes of intelligence. This is not the same as teaching our infants remarkable things to say so that they may appear to be "smart." The challenge is not how to make the baby perform to impress adults, but how to make the most of the developmental stage the child is presently in.

My Approach

My approach stems from three fundamental facts about how children form knowledge. First, babies construct knowledge by acting on the object they are trying to know. For example, to know a rattle is to know how heavy it is, how it feels, what kind of noise it makes, how it tastes, and how it smells. To know a rattle is to grasp it, shake it, smell it, mouth it. Second, children expand their knowledge by relating what they are trying to know to what they already know. Nothing is more natural than the instinct to relate the new to the old, the to-be-known to the known. If a baby already knows how to reach, grasp, and mouth objects, then he explores a new object by reaching, grasping, and mouthing! Finally, children own knowledge by using it. Once they have acted upon something and related it to their prior knowledge, they need to use it in order to master it and make it their very own. Practicing what has recently been learned is the child's way of giving some permanence to newly acquired knowledge. Although the reason for this tendency toward repetition may not always be clear to parents, the tendency itself is very familiar indeed.

We've all seen examples of this. If throwing a spoon from the high chair makes mommy pick it up once, then throwing the spoon again and again will make mommy pick it up again and again. If playing peek-a-boo the first time is fun, it is even more fun the tenth time!

Through these principles, we can see that children's knowledge develops in an orderly manner and by means of three main actions. I call the process C.E.O., which stands for:

1. **CONSTRUCT:** Children construct knowledge by acting on the things.

2. **EXPAND:** Children expand their knowledge by relating what they are trying to understand to what they already know.

3. **OWN:** Children come to own knowledge by using it.

The Enrichment Process

I have created the C.E.O. enrichment process to enable you to guide your baby's intellect. The guiding principle of this approach is to enrich the underlying processes of intellect.

In other words, we must nurture the ways of knowing—the marvelous processes of learning and understanding that are as natural as eating and drinking. Remember, to enhance the natural processes of curiosity, discovery, and inventiveness in our young children is not to hurry them along. Rather, it is to make their intellectual life more interesting, more rewarding, less frustrating, and certainly more fun.

Enriching the fundamental intellectual processes during infancy and the toddler years (and continuing to do so throughout the preschool years) sets an intellectual foundation upon which all future knowledge is based. It sharpens infants' intellectual potential and sparks their natural desire to know, leading to a lifetime of intellectual curiosity and self-motivated learning.

The purpose of educating the very young child should not be to raise a "super baby"—one who has been trained to perform specific tasks. Rather, it is to provide a supporting, encouraging, and warm environment in which the self-selected, spontaneous activities of the child are respected. And all of this should take place in an atmosphere of play, activity, and fun. We don't want to accelerate the rate at which babies attain various stages in mental development; rather, we want to influence the quality of mental activity in each stage so that the ways of knowing of each stage are completely mastered before proceeding to the next stage. Thus the brilliant, ceaseless pageant of intellect has a chance to develop to its potential prior to moving on to the other stages.

How do we do this? Well, as it turns out, the parental desire to raise "gifted" children is actually a constructive one. There are, after all, children who grow up to achieve great things. By studying the families in which such people grew up, we find that the ideas of balance and challenge we have been discussing are a major part of successful parenting.

How the Gifted Are Raised

Years ago, Professor Benjamin Bloom of the University of Chicago recently concluded an ambitious survey of 120 Americans considered to be among the top mathematicians, sculptors, neurologists, swimmers, and tennis players in the United States. He found that the single most significant factor in their development was their parents. These parents all shared four key characteristics:

1. They provided rich environments where their children explored the outside world as well as their own abilities, assuring ample opportunity for the children to initiate their own play. These parents understood that learning must take place in the act of play; that it must be fun and deeply enjoyable to the child.

2. They created wholesome surroundings with different kinds of interesting interactions for their children to explore their individual interests to the fullest and continue in their self-chosen activities. In all cases, parents served as models of motivated, determined people.

3. They encouraged their children's self-chosen interests as their own priority. Once their children reached school age, these parents continued supporting their self-initiated interests.

4. They contributed to their children's remarkable success by remaining open-minded while encouraging independent thinking and free exploration.

As parents, we should provide opportunities for our children to exercise their abilities so that they can grow to be problem-solvers, not rote learners; explorers, not mindless followers; inventors, not copiers. By developing the natural tendencies of our babies to inquire, discover, test, evaluate, search, and invent, we enable them to become independent thinkers.

Educating the Intellect

This philosophy is completely in keeping with the position taken by Piaget, and is one that I wholeheartedly endorse. The goals of education should stress independent thinking, discovery, and invention. Writing of the relation between adult society and the to-be-educated child, Piaget stated that we could no longer afford for this relationship to be unidirectional—with adult society giving out ready-made knowledge for children to absorb and repeat in the right context. "The child," he wrote, "no longer tends to approach the state of adulthood by receiving reason and the rules of right action ready-made, but by achieving them with its own effort and personal experience; in turn, society expects more of its new generation than mere imitation: it expects enrichment" (Piaget 1972b, 138).

Transmitting a set body of knowledge does not produce creative people. To improve society, the goals of education need to exceed mere repetition and imitation; they must stress independent inquiry. This emphasis is particularly crucial in view of our era of passing fads and the many pressures to conform that our children will face. The ability to be critical, to verify, to be prepared to reject the first idea that is presented if necessary—this is what we must instill in our children, and indeed in our society as a whole. To accomplish all this requires an attitude on the part of parents that puts a premium on the spontaneous activity of their children, activity that is encouraged and guided by a knowledgeable parent or caregiver.

  Knowing this fundamental difference knowledge is the best tool you have in creating an enriching experience for your baby's early intellectual development. In the next chapter, I will describe how my approach differs from some popular methods for teaching babies. Though these other techniques seem to produce impressive "results," you will see that they actually fail to stimulate your baby's underlying intellectual processes. Knowing the fundamental difference will allow you to wisely choose activities (and toys) that are best suited to your baby's needs and development.

building genius: truths, caveats, and falsehoods

Though we know so much about how babies learn, views on how to educate young children differ. Generally, ideas on this issue fall into two camps: the "active" and the "passive" ways. What I have described in the previous chapter, encouraging a baby's own exploration and invention through activity, is the active way. Unfortunately, the passive way is more commonly used, embedded in all types of learning material for babies, preschoolers, and school-aged kids.

The passive approach falls short of enhancing intellectual development. As I will explain in this chapter, this approach may be all right for learning things by rote, but it does little to enrich the minds of our children. I have taken the liberty of summarizing it for you here because I think it might make you aware of the claims that some educators, toy manufacturers, and video producers make in order to influence you to buy their products. The active and passive ways differ on three major issues:

1. How humans learn;

2. What knowledge is; and

3. What the outcomes and processes of education should be.

Let's take a quick look.

How Humans Learn

As I discussed in the previous chapter, the active way holds that children learn best by using their own abilities to act on the objects around them, assimilating the new knowledge they gather to what they already know. This view is supported not only by Piaget, but also by many subsequent research studies that we will discuss in the next chapter.

In contrast, the passive way assumes that learners are:

→ Passive, meaning that in order to learn, they must wait to be stimulated from an outside source;

→ Reactive, meaning that in order to learn they need to react to some external object, event, or idea.

This philosophy reduces human learners to sponges-creatures who learn anything best by listening, associating, repeating, and memorizing. It is as if your baby is an empty receptacle waiting to be filled with information. Thus the principal teaching technique is to bombard her with things she should know over and over again. We see this approach all the time. From a very young age, children are encouraged to memorize everything from the alphabet to multiplication tables.

This belief that humans learn best by repeating and memorizing leads to a philosophy of education that says if you keep feeding children ready-made facts and information they'll eventually absorb them. The goal is to find an efficient way of imparting information from the outside world to the child's mind. As you can see, this one-way exercise keeps the child inactive. As a matter of fact, most educators of this stripe believe that the more quiet the child can be kept, the more efficient the learning process!

At best, it is unrealistic to expect babies to sit still for this kind of teaching technique for any length of time. At worst, these techniques are often seriously out of sync with how babies learn and their intellectual attainments, especially in the earliest stages of development. Trying to force the issue can easily lead to frustration for both you and your baby!

Just as importantly, a one-note educational technique ignores the variety of ways children learn. Scientific facts and principles are acquired best through rediscovery. This makes simple sense—your baby will learn much more about what snow is by playing in it and touching it than by looking at a flash card with a picture of snow. Logical/mathematical truths are best mastered through reinvention. Imagine your baby putting toys in a basket and taking them out again to help visualize addition and subtraction, or the concepts of more and less, and you'll see what I mean. It is only conventional knowledge that is best learned through rote memorization.

What Knowledge Is

The active way holds that individuals create meaning out of their interaction with objects and ideas. On the other hand, the passive way assumes that the object of knowledge—that which we are trying to understand—has meaning of its own, independent of the knower. However, to give one example, one toddler's understanding of ball is different from another's or, better yet, different from a baby's. A baby might attempt to taste a ball or shake it to see how he can relate to it. A toddler sees a ball as something to bounce, to kick, or to throw. When a toddler learns to say "one," is his understanding of it the same as yours or a mathematician's? Obviously not! A toddler's idea of one is limited, whereas yours is more mature. When my two-year-old son Jeremy wants to indicate "more," he says "big." These are just simple examples.

To take it to another level, obviously you and I can look at the same picture, witness an event, watch a movie and can—and do—abstract different meanings from them. This is simply because our current stage of development, coupled with our previous knowledge, experience, and know-how of these things are different. One child might delight when she is introduced to another child, whereas another may be very shy and reserved when encountering strangers. Neither response is wrong; they are merely individual. Reducing meaning to a one-size-fits all proposition limits the alternatives your child might otherwise discover for herself. As you see, the passive approach forgets that meaning resides in people, not in things.

The Outcomes and Processes of Education

The active way shies away from trying to rigidly measure what children have learned, because learning is a process that ideally never stops. The passive way, however, insists that the outcomes of instruction must be measurable in order for teaching to be effective. For example: Can a two-year-old name colors or count to three? Can a three-year-old recite the alphabet? Can a four-year-old tell you how much two plus two equals? This kind of yes or no checklist easily measures what children "know."

So what's wrong with this approach? The problem is that it emphasizes outcomes of instruction at the expense of processes of thought. There is nothing wrong with teaching our young children these tasks, provided that the process doesn't end there. What we have to do is go to the next level—to engage our children in processes that build intelligence. Instead of simply teaching a twenty-two-month-old the colors of the plastic balls she loves playing with, we can also group all the yellow ones here, all the red ones there, or all the big ones here, all the small ones there. This activity introduces a fundamental process of mathematics: categorizing things, which will eventually lead to classification and, later on, to set theory.

In other words, I can teach my children to associate a certain thing (an orange ball) with a certain word (orange). And if we repeat the names of the colors and match them with the right color balls, they will soon learn the colors. Learning to name colors is an important part of acquiring conventional knowledge. But why stop there? We can discover the physical properties of the balls (are they light or heavy? do they bounce? are they rough or smooth?) and we can invent a thing or two with them (line them up, arrange them in circles, compare them to large balls or small balls, compare them to blocks, categorize them, count them, etc.).

When you engage your baby in these processes of thought, you are literally engaging her mind. Conversely, if you think only of teaching kids to say the right answer without understanding how that answer was reached, you may be short-changing the intellectual process. Processes are more difficult than outcomes to engage children in. Processes, of course, are not easily measurable, either! Here's a simple example. If you ask a child to tell you how much two plus two is, and she says four, we can easily measure the result and say that she is right. But if we were to inquire a little deeper into what she understands by this answer, we might be surprised. If we then ask this child to tell us what two plus three is, and she responds that she has not learned that yet, clearly her knowledge is superficial. It suggests that her response was learned by rote.

Intelligence and IQ

How does this distinction make a difference in intellectual development? The answer comes down to this: Rote learning might get us the right answer, but it doesn't help us to understand. We won't be able to relate such memorized knowledge to new situations or manipulate it in creative ways to solve new problems. How can this type of information contribute to intellectual development? Yet sometimes this rote knowledge is what contributes to a high IQ score! Does that mean that IQ tests are not accurate measures of intelligence? Absolutely!

When we speak of intelligence, we generally think of ways of testing children that give us a quick measurement of their learning. In fact, we are often just measuring what they were able to remember. We forget that the underlying processes are what speak to what is really known.

The real challenge is how to avoid imposing teaching schemes on our babies that make them learn meaninglessly. If we don't pay attention to the way that children learn and

make meaning naturally, then we run the risk that they will
end up hating the very act of learning.

In fact, this is why so many children dislike school-they
don't see any meaning in what they are told to learn. For
example, if your preschooler recites the Pledge of Allegiance
and uses the word "indivisible," does she know what that
means? And how well do children retain information learned
merely by repetition? Most of it is soon forgotten. The reason is simple. What was supposedly learned was not related
to what she already knew about the subject. It was simply
memorized for the purpose of blurting out when the right
question was asked.

A famous psychologist, William James, once visited a fifth-
grade class. The teacher asked the class, "In what state is
the center of the earth?" to which the class responded

in unison: "In the state of igneous fusion." He wondered whether the children had any notion of what their answer meant, so he politely requested permission to ask the children a question. The teacher agreed, and James asked, "Children, if I were to strap you to your chair and dangle you down through a hole in this classroom all the way to the core of the earth, how would you feel: would you feel cold, hot, or the same?" There was utter silence. He repeated the question and got the same result: deafening silence! Uncomfortable about the ignorance displayed by her class, the teacher repeated her original question: "In what state is the center of the earth?" to which the class joyfully responded: "In the state of igneous fusion."

Popularizing the Traditional

In recent years, the passive way has moved out of the classroom and can now be found in a variety of methods and products claiming to build a smarter baby. A few you may be familiar with are:

→ Flash cards
→ Reading to baby
→ Developmental toys

Though advocates of these methods may make sweeping claims for their products, none of these ideas qualifies as a developmentally sound way of enriching a baby's intellectual development.

FLASH CARDS

Flash cards are used to train infants to point to a named object or, later, to name the object on the card. In addition, to teach math to infants, flash cards with varying numbers of dots on them are prepared. Babies are shown a pair of such cards at a time, one that has a few dots on it and one that has many more. Babies are then asked to point to the one that has more. When the baby is able to comply, it is said that she has learned a mathematical fact. This method is very popular and easy.

An Extreme Example

Some authors promote this flash-card method for infants for all types of learning. Glenn Doman, a physical therapist by training, is the leading proponent of this method. Doman recommends teaching infants to read and to recognize written numbers so that they may acquire a vast vocabulary for identifying things in their surroundings and learn math. Parents are told that there is no inherent difference between their baby and any other baby, not even a baby Mozart or baby Michelangelo. They are told that Michelangelo distinguished himself because he learned more facts than the average person.

According to Doman the accumulation of facts determines genius. Therefore, his reasoning goes, the cornerstone of educational programs for the very young, including infants, should be the teaching of specific facts. And because the most efficient way to acquire facts is through the printed word, we must teach our infants to read, teach them vocabulary and number skills. For example, babies are taught to "read" words such as "mommy," "daddy," and "spaghetti," written on flash cards and presented in rapid succession. The process is repeated day in and day out until the baby learns to "read." In this approach, reading is viewed as the critical means in advancing the intelligence of very young children. Since facts constitute the building blocks of intelligence, it is argued that parents can, in effect, create geniuses of their babies by teaching them facts, reading, and number skills.

Beyond the Super Baby Syndrome

The widespread acceptance of these ideas may have more to do with our latent feelings of guilt than with any sound cognitive theory. Parents certainly would never knowingly deprive their children of those skills identified as the building blocks of intelligence. The super baby approach takes an active tone—teach, and teach early—so to ignore it is to do nothing, and rob our children of potential advantage later in life! But the real question is not whether early interaction is helpful—that we know with virtual certainty—but how valid the ideas supporting this particular theory really are.

Even the most cursory look at scientific findings shows the super baby notion to be terribly simplistic and profoundly flawed. If teaching facts early on were the only factor in determining intellectual competence, what a different world we would live in! What a simple matter it would be to fill our schools with future Nobel laureates!

Little is gained if a child knows which of two cards has more dots on it or turns out to be the first on the block to speak or read. If these things happen without prodding, fine. It is pointless to push your baby into artificial learning situations, situations that emphasize achievement based on rote learning. Young children pay too high an emotional price when they are rushed into achieving tasks that are inappropriate for their current stage of development.

READING TO BABY

Just recently, I attended a luncheon with a small group of highly successful businessmen. My good friend introduced me to the group, saying that I had written a book about the intellectual development of infants. One of the gentlemen immediately said, "Reading! All you have to do is read to them." He quickly asked me to concur with him, asking, "Isn't that true? I seem to have read that somewhere." He was initially shocked when I disagreed with him. However, as I explained that reading is too abstract an act, involving symbols the baby has no way of grasping, he began to agree.

For many, like my new acquaintance, intelligence is synonymous with the ability to use words. The mistake we so often make is to equate a baby's intelligence with the ability to speak, and later, with the ability to read and write. Reading and writing often take on disproportionate importance in the way we evaluate the very early development of the child.

Some parents have been convinced that constant reading to their babies, and even their unborn children, is important to future development. Somehow the unborn baby is supposed to absorb this extremely complex symbolic activity even before she is born! The less zealous protagonists of reading to unborn babies claim that at least the fetus is getting used to your voice. There is some truth to this notion, but your everyday conversation alone does the trick quite nicely!

Reading to an unborn child is, quite simply, an utter waste of time. Better to spend time preparing for her arrival, learning about her physical development, and attending to your own physical, nutritional, and psychological condition. Once she is born, you should concentrate on providing love, care, and social and mental interaction. But young babies have no words. They have perceptions and actions. And it is through these perceptions and actions, and especially combinations of these, that they construct knowledge of what things are.

Much later on, reading takes on great significance. It enables your child to speed up mental processes and accomplish actions symbolically, as opposed to through direct action. It enables the mind to soar, to imagine objects and events that are not physically present to the reader, and thus it frees the mind from the confines of the here and now. So reading is important, but not in infancy.

By all means introduce your baby to books, but don't be disappointed if she shows little interest in being read to, or if she would rather chew on a book than look at it. Be patient. After eighteen months or so, and certainly by her second birthday, when her ability to understand words and symbols has begun to mature, she will almost certainly be more eager to enjoy a book with you.

DEVELOPMENTAL TOYS

More recently, the market has been flooded with so-called developmental toys. You might wonder what makes these toys "developmental," and I encourage you to examine these claims critically, as some have little basis.

For instance, research has clearly shown that babies prefer to look at contrasts and contours and at bold stripes. Consequently, many new developmental infant toys stress bold colors, striking stripes, and contrasting polka dots. Unfortunately, some don't seem to have any reason for calling their toy "developmental" except for it being finished with these features.

I see at least two problems with this: first, from your baby's point of view, the toy is attractive, but if it does not engage her beyond that, she will quickly drop it. Second, this isolated finding, while true, can be misleading. An undue emphasis on this one fact of early development gives it more importance than it probably deserves. Baby toys should be based on comprehensive theories and findings pertaining to those theories, not isolated scientific facts.

Of course, I chose to talk about toys here only to point out how parents can be influenced by trends stemming from one isolated piece of information. We all want to do what's best for our babies, and manufacturers can take advantage of that desire. Buying the right toy at the right time is of course important for your baby. More important is that parenting suggestions like this one should be based on a conceptual framework that shows parents how what they're doing fits within an overall picture of development.

We would all love to know a simple formula to turn our children into geniuses. The evidence shows, however, that the Michelangelos and Mozarts of the world do differ in profound ways from the rest of us. Any recipe for creating genius purely through the force-feeding of facts and figures denies the exquisitely complicated interaction between the child's innate abilities (nature) and her surroundings (nurture). The key to understanding cognitive development is to recognize the inescapable reality of this interaction. As we will see throughout this book, the real challenge is to identify the cognitive stage that your baby is in and try and match a stage-appropriate activity with it. There is no baby on earth exactly like yours and there is no substitute for identifying your baby's current ways of knowing and matching them with meaningful interactions between your baby and the thing she is trying to learn.

Super baby training programs, as we have seen, teach babies to respond in specific ways to specific stimulus situations. Unfortunately, training babies to perform these kinds of tasks is useless. It is extremely seductive, though; it lulls parents into believing that their child has mastered something that will advance her intelligence. But this kind of learning tends to be short-lived and is of no consequence in your baby's overall future intellectual development.

For example, one three year-old boy impressed adults with his ability to "read" the words "booster rocket" while pointing to a picture of one. The fact that the child can make this association means nothing in terms of what has been learned. No one would suggest that this youngster knows a thing about the principles of rocketry, boosters, or stellar navigation!

We refer to such instances of learning as empty verbalisms—words devoid of meaning. Equipping children with empty verbalisms may impress the uninitiated parent and the "audience," but it is a meaningless, useless form of learning.

Or consider the one-year-old son of a colleague of mine. Once I accompanied both of them on a summer motor trip of several hundred miles; my friend kept pointing to cows grazing in the countryside and repeating the word "cow." He believed that if a word were repeated and associated with the object it represented over and over again, a child could actually learn that word's meaning. My friend must have pointed and repeated the word "cow" dozens of times. When we reached our destination, the child looked at his father's index finger. "Cow!" he said proudly.

Yes: children can learn simple associations between words and objects. However, we should not be concerned with equipping babies with end results, ready-made facts, or simple associations. Babies learn best when they act on the objects that they are trying to learn about. When we focus solely on eliciting the desired response, we run the risk of stifling our babies' creativity and their natural desire to discover. Fortunately, familiarizing yourself with the various stages of development will not only allow you to avoid the common pitfalls of traditional educational methods; they will also allow you to appreciate the natural signs of your baby's developing intelligence.

as the twig is bent, so grows the tree

You may be wondering how we know that the first two years are so critical for your baby's cognitive development. First, science tells us that your baby's unparalleled early brain growth opens windows of learning opportunities that set the stage for much of his future development. By the age of three, his brain forms approximately 1000 trillion cell connections. Secondly, early experience literally changes the physiology of the brain, thereby determining the brain's ability to function. This means that what you do in these critical first few years will impact your baby's intellect in a

profound way. Thirdly, studies of the effects of early enrichment, or deprivation, show us both the benefits and detrimental effects that environment can have on your baby's
development. And finally, to develop properly, a baby's brain
needs certain types of experience at critical periods, making
the correct timing of those experiences essential to your
baby's future cognitive development.

Brain Cells and Connections

Your baby starts out as a single cell. But during the next
nine months, he grows so rapidly that, at birth, his brain
contains about one hundred billion cells. Though brain
growth is unsurpassed during the prenatal period, only
one-sixth of the brain develops before birth. It is difficult to
imagine anything growing at the rate of the human brain
during the early years. While the fetus is still in the womb,
approximately twenty-five thousand brain cells are produced each minute!

Though brain size is important, it is not the whole story.
Cells in the nervous system (neurons) do not actually
touch each other. When stimulated, neurons fire, releasing
chemicals that cross the tiny gaps (synapses) to neighbor-
ing neurons. In this way, they send messages to each other,
building networks of connections that form the structure of
the brain.

Every time your baby experiences an event or performs
an action, the affected brain areas activate and connect to

one another to make sense of the entire incident. Memories of these sensory and action episodes are stored and transmitted to other networks. The more your baby experiences, the more complex these networks become, enabling him to function in increasingly novel, varied, and elaborate ways.

Brain Growth Is Most Rapid During the Early Years

In the early years, the brain grows faster than any other part of the body. That's why your baby's head is so much bigger than the rest of his body. Your brain weighs about 3.3 pounds, while your newborn's brain weighs only one-quarter of that, slightly less than a pound. In the first two years, the brain produces thousands of trillions of connections between neurons, or one hundred to one thousand connections for each of the 100 billion neurons! Yet, of the five-sixths of all connections that develop after birth, nearly three-quarters form during the first two years of life!

As you can see, the sheer gain in brain weight over the first five years is amazing:

→ By six months, your baby's brain weighs about half of what it will weigh when he becomes an adult;

→ By two years, it weighs three-quarters of what it will weigh in adult hood;

→ And by five years, it achieves ninety percent of its adult weight.

You may ask: if no more neurons are produced over baby's lifespan, what grows in baby's brain that makes it weigh so much more in adulthood? Actually, two things: First, as we've seen, the number of synaptic connections between neurons multiplies by leaps and bounds. The other factor is the breathtaking growth of something called glial cells. These cells do not transmit information. Rather, their function is to coat and insulate the nerve fibers, strengthening them and enabling them to communicate faster. This coating process is called myelination. Without the proper amount of myelination, the body could not function, not even to carry out the simplest of tasks, like crawling. Myelination occurs over many years, with some parts of the brain being myelinated earlier than others. Some parts don't get myelinated until the teenage years.

Thanks to recent technological developments, such as EEGs (electroencephalographs), PET scans (positron emission tomography) and functional magnetic resonance imaging (fMRI), which measures blood flow and oxygenation to various areas of the brain, we can tell a lot about the brain as it experiences events over time. We can pinpoint the area or areas of the brain that are activated by a certain experience, and which areas interact with each other. For example, we now know which areas of the brain are involved when we listen to music, solve math problems, knit a sweater, and so on.

In addition, we can tell how busy the brain is. For example, we can tell whether the brain of a one-year-old is more active than that of a two-year-old. This has led to an intriguing discovery about the "terrible twos." It turns out that the brain of a two-year-old is as busy as yours and mine. But that's not the most surprising part. The brain of a three-year-old is twice as busy as that of a two-year-old!

Use It or Lose It—The Way of the Brain

Once connected, neurons continue to need activity–some sort of interaction with the outside world–to stay alive; otherwise, they die off. It is precisely because of this pruning process that you and I, as adults, have fewer neurons than babies do! The old adage "use it or lose it" has never been truer! But fear not, all is not lost! If we continue to provide our brains with mental and physical activity, especially learning to do new things, playing challenging new games, reading, and problem solving, we will continue to establish new brain connections and strengthen the old ones. So let's not only keep our babies active; let's stay active as well! It is a win/win situation.

How important is keeping our brains busy? To answer this question we need only turn to nature itself. Even in sleep, the brain is actively sorting things–taking things apart and putting them back together. In fact, studies have shown that the brain is busier during sleep than during waking hours!

Taking things apart and reconnecting them together-making sense-is the hallmark of brain activity.

Since neuronal complexity increases at such an astounding rate in the first two years, enriching, stage-appropriate activities during this time are critical. Conversely, it follows that if a baby is neglected during this critical time, he will suffer irreparable damage, as shown by much animal as well as human research. For example, a landmark experiment by Hubel and Weisel in 1970 showed that month-old kittens deprived of light for only three to four days showed degeneration in the visual centers of the brain. Other neuroscientists, such as Diamond in 1990, have shown that rats trained to run mazes of increasing complexity developed thicker cerebral cortices than rats that did not receive such training. These researchers were also able to show that rats raised in enriched environments that contained ladders, exercise wheels, and mazes also developed thicker cortical layers than rats raised without these "toys." However, in order for the rats to benefit, these toys had to be changed at least twice a week! Undoubtedly, active experience enhances brain growth, both in size and complexity, especially when there is variety in the type of experience.

Does this apply to humans as well? Neuroscientists as a whole believe the answer is a definite "yes." For example, in 1990 Arnold Scheibel examined the brains of two gifted individuals: a world-class violinist and a distinguished artist.

He noticed that the primary auditory region of the violinist was twice as thick as the average individual, while the artist's primary visual cortex was much thicker than that of a normal individual.

Brains and Computers

Some people liken the brain to a computer. This interesting comparison can teach us a lot. On the one hand, the brain, like a computer, is equipped with hardware (the neurons) and software (it is programmed to develop properly given a supporting environment). Unlike a computer however-which is completely wired, ready to work, but with its limits established by its hardware-the human brain starts with some wiring and an internal guiding mechanism that makes it build itself as it is used. The brain is a unique kind of computer, to continue the analogy. As a matter of fact, the brain begins working well before birth and certainly before it is finished being wired. In other words, your baby's brain works as it develops, and develops as it works. For example, it is certainly not like a computer in that today's computers don't and can't change their memory capacity. Your baby's brain grows as it is being used, shaping its very nature through its own activity. This activity changes the structure of the brain itself.

With this in mind, imagine what happens to brain activity when there is little stimulation or enrichment at all. As you might guess, a sterile environment will produce a diminished amount of brain activity, resulting in an inferior brain structure. Conversely, enriched environments influence your baby's brain positively, increasing activity that helps to form more elaborate connections and a more complex stucture.

Brain Growth and Baby Actions

The emergence of new capabilities depends on brain growth; that is, brain growth makes the emergence of certain actions possible. As active experience changes the structure of your baby's brain, he will develop new abilities. To show how this process works, neuroscientists have been able to find correlations between brain connections (synaptic formation) and human action. Here are some examples:

→ At two months, the motor area of the brain begins to form connections. At this age infants lose their startle and rooting reflexes—meaning that as they begin to exert some degree of control over these functions, their actions become voluntary rather than strictly reflexive.

→ At three months, cell formation peaks in the occipital area, which is the seat of vision. The result: your baby's eyes can now focus not only at eight to ten inches from his nose but at greater and lesser distances as well.

→ At eight or nine months, the hippocampus becomes fully functional. Result: your baby can form explicit memories.

→ Between six and twelve months, the prefrontal cortex, the seat of forethought and logic, forms synapses at a furi ous rate, so much so that it consumes twice the energy of an entire adult brain. The consequence: Your baby can now understand the concepts of object permanence, cause and effect, and means-ends, among others.

→ By twelve months, your baby's auditory map is formed. The result: He can now pick up new phonemes or language sounds at an amazing rate.

→ It has been well established that the left hemisphere is heavily involved in language development. At about two years of age, the neural branching in the language region of the left hemisphere of a child's brain grows at an astounding rate, just when language comprehension and expression begin to explode.

Beyond what we know of the physical development of the human brain, a number of studies, conducted on both animals and humans, examine how early experience affects the growth of the brain and its soul partner, the mind. Examining the results of these studies has two benefits. First, they reiterate the enormous impact of early experience on cognitive development; and second, they help us learn about the process of enrichment, nurturance, and love of very young children so that we can be better coaches during this fascinating and critical time.

Only recently have we begun to grasp the full impact of early experience upon later development, although psychologists have speculated about it for over seventy years.

This knowledge, which comes to us from the exciting new fields of psychobiology and neuropsychology, confirms our earlier speculations that the early years are crucial to future intellectual development.

We can now point to a number of research areas that clearly support the importance of early experience in brain growth and intellectual development, including animal enrichment and deprivation, studies of orphaned children and malnourished babies, and early intervention. Let's examine each of these areas.

An Animal Study or Two: To Enrich or Not to Enrich?

ENRICHED BRAINS WEIGH MORE

A classic set of animal experiments performed by Professor David Krech of the University of California at Berkeley studied the role of early experience on later development using laboratory rats taken from the same litter and randomly divided into two groups. One group was placed in an "enriched" environment: cages with wheels that could be turned, little tunnels to run through, and things to climb over, under, around, and through. These rats were also allowed to explore new territories outside their cages for thirty minutes a day. The other group had none of these things. In every other respect the two groups were treated equally. Three months later, both groups were sacrificed in order to explore their brains. The result was fascinating: the brains of the enriched group weighed more, had more curvatures, and contained a certain enzyme called acetylcholinesterase known to be linked to learning, remembering, and problem-solving. The smaller brains of the non-enriched group lacked this learning enzyme!

Enriched Brains Learn Faster

Professor Bernard Hymovitch conducted a sequel to that experiment, in which he provided enriching experiences to rats of different ages. In his experiment, however, after the initial treatment period was over, the rats were not sacrificed; instead, they were given a kind of "rat intelligence test" in which they had to run a maze to obtain food. Two results were immediately clear: The enriched groups learned the maze much faster than the non-enriched groups, and the younger the rats had been when the enrichment was introduced the more beneficial the outcome! In addition, Hymovitch documented the importance of the type of enrichment used and showed that stimulus variety is directly related to future intellectual development.

Sterile Environments Produce Fewer Cell Connections

Just recently, University of Illinois researchers showed that the brains of laboratory rats confined to sterile, uninteresting boxes contain up to twenty-five percent fewer connections per cell.

Maternal Deprivation Causes Cells to Die Off

Reporting on animal studies, Mark Smith of the Dupont Merck Research Labs shows that severe maternal deprivation early in life causes an animal's brain cells to die off at twice the rate of animals raised by their mothers. Researchers are convinced that touch is the key ingredient here. Consistent with our natural parenting tendencies, research underscores the fact that a mother's (or a caring adult's) loving touch is critical to healthy emotional and mental development.

These classic experiments serve to illustrate the impact of an engaging environment on growth and development in the very early phases of life. Interaction with an interesting and stimulating environment as early as possible has a definite beneficial effect on brain development, which in turn promotes the ability to learn. The best summary of our present state of knowledge on this subject is a simple one: Active early experience is the key to future intellectual growth.

Human Studies: Examining Different Experiences

ORPHANED CHILDREN FALL BEHIND

Even if enrichment during infancy helps baby rats to develop into better and faster learners, how do we know that enrichment in human infants also makes difference? To answer this question, we turn to studies of neglected orphans. In one of the oldest and most noteworthy studies, Dr. Wayne Dennis studied children raised in an orphanage in Tehran, Iran where very little human contact, to say nothing of mental enrichment, was offered. Although these children had freedom of movement, they lacked stimulus variety—they had little or no interaction with toys, animals, or people. When Dr. Dennis discovered these children, they had been left alone in this sterile environment practically all their lives. The result was a disaster:

→ Sixty percent of them could not sit up alone until they were two years old.

→ Eighty-five percent could not walk until age four!

Obviously, these conditions were quite extreme. Nonetheless, this chilling example graphically illustrates the impact that lack of enrichment can have on development.

More recently, in 1998 neuroscientist Mary Carlson of Harvard University was able to substantiate these findings using PET scans of the brains of Romanian orphans who were institutionalized shortly after birth. Like the Iranian orphans studied by Dr. Dennis, these orphans grew up without the benefit of parental attention–they weren't touched, caressed, or played with. They simply existed in the most sterile of environments, with little or no interaction with adults. The results are truly enlightening yet heartbreaking.

The orphaned child's temporal lobes, the circled areas, are devoid of activity, whereas the normal child's temporal lobes show plenty of activity. It is precisely these areas of the brain that are wired with cell connections through experience in the early years. (To enable the newborn to survive through simple perceptions and reflex actions, the brain stem and other primitive areas are the only structures that are wired at birth. The rest has to be wired with experience). Children raised in severely neglected conditions end up with this kind of brain deficit, and end up suffering both emotional and cognitive problems.

THE EFFECT OF POOR-QUALITY DAY CARE

Carlson's next finding is even more alarming. She studied young children who were left in poor-quality day-care centers. The children she observed had abnormally high levels of a stress hormone known as cortisol on weekdays but not on weekends, when they were with their parents.

It turns out that children with high levels of cortisol tend to do poorly on motor and mental ability tests. Moreover, the areas of the brain (temporal lobes) that receive input from the senses and regulate emotions had little, if any, activity. This deficit resulted in emotional problems and deficits in mental ability later on in life.

Also, in August 2000 a report on sudden infant death syndrome (SIDS) showed that twenty percent of all incidents of SIDS occurred in poor-quality day-care centers, as compared to seven percent in ordinary homes.

CHILDREN WHO DON'T PLAY MUCH HAVE SMALLER BRAINS

Just recently Baylor College of Medicine scientists were able to show that children who don't play much or who are rarely touched develop brains that are twenty to thirty percent smaller than normal for their age. The evidence is once again clear: sterile environments result in brain deficits that affect intellectual development. Very young children who are neglected or abused bear scars that are difficult if not impossible to overcome.

The question remains open: Is this finding due to lack of interaction with caring adults? I think so. To sum it all up, poor early experiences produce poor brains; conversely, rich early experiences produce rich and inquisitive brains.

EARLY NURTURING MEANS BETTER LIFELONG HEALTH

Even more recently, in 2004 a team of researchers from the University of Albany and the University of Michigan found that the more children are nurtured by their parents, the more likely they are to remain physically and mentally healthy through old age. Analyzing a 1995–1996 survey of three thousand adults, the researchers found that survey participants who hadn't gotten enough emotional support from their parents were not only more likely to suffer from depression or other emotional illness, they were also more likely to report poorer physical health. Most surprising was how long the connection seemed to last; the participants ranged in age from twenty-five to seventy-four. Ultimately, this means that the love you give your baby will help his cognitive development now and promote his health and well-being throughout his life.

MALNOURISHED CHILDREN DO NOT REACH FULL POTENTIAL

In his comprehensive book The Brain: The Last Frontier, Richard M. Restak writes: "The brains of children who have died of malnutrition during the first year of life have fewer brain cells compared to normal children. They also have an overall decrease in whole brain size. In addition, it seems not to make much difference exactly when malnutrition occurs, as long as it's sometime in the first two years" (129). Dr. Restak, citing the work of Dr. Ernesto Pollitt of the Massachusetts Institute of Technology with Native American children, states that Pollitt "demonstrated a 50 per cent decrease in behavioral performance in severely malnourished children. Memory, abstract reasoning, thinking, and verbal ability were most affected" (128). Based on observations of a group of Korean children who were adopted in the U.S. and who had been severely malnourished early in life, Dr. Merrill S. Read of the National Institute of Child Health and Human Development concludes: "'[M]alnutritioned children, even though they are not retarded in later life, are never able to achieve their full intellectual potential'" (Restak 130).

How widespread is malnutrition among young children? Once again, Restak, citing a study by the World Health Organization, states that as many as three hundred million children worldwide are undernourished. Malnourished young children are at risk of suffering from a significant decrease in mental processes such as thinking, reasoning, and memory later on in life. Even subsequent good nutrition cannot fully make up for early deprivation.

Is this question merely academic for you and me, since our children are most likely, and fortunately, not in this category? Or does this have a practical implication for us as well? We as parents can profoundly affect our child's health and nutrition even before birth. A pregnant woman who smokes, drinks, does drugs, survives on junk food, or lives with prolonged periods of stress or depression risks harm to her unborn baby. By safeguarding her own health, she protects her child's. When our babies are born, we have another important choice to make. Studies show that breast-fed babies tend to score higher on tests of intelligence than formula-fed babies. And finally, when our children begin to eat solid food, we must teach them sensible, healthy eating habits. In short, though our children are not at risk of starvation, our choices can help our children begin life in the best possible position to learn and grow.

Early Intervention: Start Early, Start Right

For over thirty years, we have had evidence suggesting that early intervention makes a difference. One study in 1971 started it all. In the ghettos of Milwaukee, Wisconsin, educa-

tional psychologists trained mothers of a group of newborns
to play with and care for their babies in ways that would
help their babies develop intellectually. At four months of
age, the babies were brought to The Milwaukee Young Children Education Center and engaged in a variety of activities specifically designed to promote mental development.
These babies were later compared with a group of babies
born and raised in the same ghetto but who simply, and
unfortunately, were not included in the study. The second
group was comparable in age and health, yet their mothers
had not received instruction in how to enrich the mental life
of their babies, nor did the babies attend the school. The
findings were startling. By age two, the enriched group had
surpassed the non-enriched group significantly in every
facet of intellect. By age four, these differences were even
more pronounced! Further, even after the children were ten
years old, the differences between the enriched and the
non-enriched groups were still very evident.

The Milwaukee Project is one of many studies producing
these astounding results. Ever-mounting evidence confirms
the fact that early intervention in the lives of children has a
lasting effect on their future success. A thorough reexami-
nation of the old Head Start Program started in 1965, which
had been labeled a dismal failure, was recently completed
at the Perry Preschool Program of Ypsilanti, Michigan. The
study shows that children who had entered the program
when they were three and four years old demonstrated sig-

nificant benefit from their earlier training when they were evaluated some nineteen years later. They showed substantial improvements in school success, social responsibility, and socioeconomic success over their counterparts who had not participated in the program. Interestingly, the early advantage participants showed in intelligence test scores was the only difference that did not persist, a fact the study attributes to the relatively late age (three or four) at which the children entered the program. Once again, indisputable evidence substantiates the wisdom of starting enrichment as early as possible.

In 1998 Barnett reviewed thirty-eight studies on the long-term effects of early intervention (before the age of five) on cognitive functions or school success through third grade of children in poverty, and found the following general patterns:

1. Gains in IQ resulting from intervention beginning in kindergarten tend to fade rapidly upon entry into elementary school. However, gains realized from intervention beginning at least in the first year of life tend to persist well into adolescence.

2. In contrast to IQ scores, the effects of early intervention on achievement scores do not fade out; they tend to persist well into the high school years.

3. Early intervention shows a uniformly positive effect on school success, as measured by grade retention, need for special education, and rate of high school graduation.

Michael J. Guralnick of the University of Washington reviewed the data on the effectiveness of early intervention for children at risk and for those with established disabilities, and concluded: "Early intervention may well be the centerpiece in our nation's efforts on behalf of vulnerable children and their families" (337).

In a recent article summarizing the effectiveness of a comprehensive, five-year program of early childhood intervention for low-income children, Barbara D. Goodson and associates (2000) state: "Three linked hypotheses—that the child's early development lays the foundation for his or her long-term functioning, that early environmental influences have important effects on early development, and that poverty is associated with a variety of material and psychological deficits in children's early experiences—are widely accepted, supported by research evidence, and have troubling implications" (5).

Upon reviewing the literature, Frank Newman, president of the Education Commission of the States, concludes: "There is a time scale to brain development, and the most important year is the first" (Nash 51). Well-designed preschool programs can help many children overcome deficits in their homes.

The best summary of our present state of knowledge on this subject is a simple one: The quantity, quality, and variety of early experience is the key to future intellectual growth. No other time span is more important to the development of intellectual structures or functions than the first two years. Early, stage-appropriate enriching experience is of critical importance in bolstering a child's development potential. Loving adults, who raise young children in nurturing and predictable settings, bring up children who are more intelligent than children who are raised by parents who are inattentive and who don't provide a loving, secure environment. Neglected children suffer serious—sometimes irreversible—behavioral and intellectual setbacks, while systematic intervention in infants who are raised in poverty and who seem doomed to failure makes a big difference in their intellectual prowess.

what newborns know

In previous chapters I have hinted at the amazing abilities of newborns. In this chapter I will tell you about the host of abilities your baby possesses from the moment of birth. Newborns are not the incompetent, passive, reactive creatures some may assume they are; rather, they are active knowledge-seeking, knowledge-making, know-how-inventing creatures. Once again, the experiences that they have during the early years will have a telling effect how these abilities develop.

Introduction

Many parents don't expect much from their newborns. They believe that a child has to experience things over a long time before she can begin to sense, much less to know anything. Some even believe that newborns can't see, hear, feel, taste, or smell. As a matter of fact, even today, there are some self-appointed experts who consider newborns to be helpless, incompetent creatures who arrive in this world unprepared, passive, and unintelligent. They see babies as empty receptacles waiting to be literally stuffed with knowledge.

Actually, babies are able to function in remarkable ways from birth. The reflexes and perceptions that they are born with serve them quite well. These sensorimotor systems enable them to adapt to the world around them in some limited yet functional ways. For example, when a bulky object like a box is pushed toward them, newborns only a few days old will thrust their heads back and raise their hands to protect their faces.

The pages that follow are filled with fascinating information, just like the reaction described above. I've tried to select interesting and relevant experiments to illustrate the marvelous abilities of the human newborn.

The 1960s and 1970s saw a sudden surge of research into what and how babies know. Since then, psychologists have improved their techniques for studying newborns and how parents interact with them. While Piaget's theory remains the most comprehensive and detailed theory of how infants construct knowledge, psychologists have recently shown that some infant abilities, especially facial imitations, manifest themselves earlier than Piaget had theorized.

Still, the resulting picture says three things: (a) newborns are much more intelligent than we ever thought they'd be, (b) they can learn things quickly and easily if we know what to do and when to do it, and (c) what makes them unique is the type of experience they have in the early years. Let's now take a panoramic view of the landscape of a newborn's world of knowledge and know-how—what she knows about things and people and what abilities she has.

Knowing What Babies Know

How do we know what babies know? Psychologists have developed a few techniques to help them answer this question. First, we observe them in their natural setting. For example, how long do they sleep, and how long do they stay awake? Second, we observe their reaction to different kinds of stimulation. What do they do when you shine a weak light in their eyes? What do they do when you snap your fingers? Do they turn their head in the direction of the sound? When we make faces, stick our tongues or open our mouths wide, do they imitate us? How old are they when they do these things? Third, we can capitalize on the fact that newborns, like the rest of us, get bored when they experience the same thing over and over again. If you play a note or show a picture to a newborn over and over again, the baby will get bored and lose interest in it. This is what we call habituation. Dishabituation is, of course, just the opposite. It refers to renewed interest in something. So if we show a baby a happy face over and over again, she will show less and less interest in it. If we then show her a sad face, and she perks up, we know that she can tell the difference between the happy face and the sad face. This is an important tool in studying newborns. And it can be used to test virtually all the senses. Fourth, we can use the amount of time that newborns do something as an indication of their abilities. So if we show them two things, such as a happy face and a sad face, and they spend more time looking at the happy one, we know that they can tell the difference between the two faces and that they prefer the happy face to the sad one.

Using these techniques, developmental psychologists have been able to map out a whole host of newborn competencies. Here are some of the most important ones.

Your Newborn's Motor Skills

Your baby is born with a working motor system that is the basis of much of her future learning and development. At the heart of this system is a set of survival reflexes including crying, sound making, sneezing, coughing, sucking, eye movements (blinking, focusing, tracking), grasping, and swallowing. Objects and events in your baby's surroundings trigger these actions. If, for example, you stroke a newborn's cheek or the area near her mouth with your hand, her head turns and her tongue moves toward your hand. Once she finds your hand, she begins sucking. Or, if you shine a small light into her eyes, or clap your hands in front of her face, she will close her eyes tightly.

Your Newborn's Sensory Skills

A newborn's senses are developed well enough to enable her to survive and learn. Here's a brief summary of what your baby senses from the moment she is born.

VISION

While her vision is blurry, a newborn can see pretty well as long as the object is about ten inches from her nose. This is how Mother Nature designed it. After all, this is exactly where her mother's face is when she breastfeeds her. As a matter of fact, a newborn knows her mommy's face and prefers it to strange ones.

HEARING

Hearing is functional even before birth. After two or three days a newborn's hearing is good enough to make out different voices, and it keeps improving well into the elementary school years. A newborn's hearing is especially sensitive to human voices. In fact, she can even discriminate familiar voices from strange ones and prefers the familiar.

SMELL

The sense of smell is also functional at birth. Experiments show that newborns sense the same odors that adults do. Furthermore, they often, but not always, have the same likes and dislikes as adults. Any early differences seem to disappear by the time they reach three years old.

TASTE

Newborns respond to all four basic tastes: sweet, sour, bitter, and salty. It is also well established that they prefer sweet to the other tastes.

TOUCH

Actually, touch differs from the rest of the senses in that it really consists of many sensations: temperature, pain, pressure, and vibration. A newborn responds to all of these sensations.

Right Brain, Left Brain

The human brain is a wondrous instrument. Research into the relation between the brain and intellectual development has given us important insight into the cognitive preferences of babies. The two hemispheres, or halves, of the brain are organized to function in different ways. The right hemisphere specializes in processing information in a simultaneous way, while the left processes it in a sequential or linear way. Speaking and counting are examples of a linear thought process; perception and music are examples of simultaneous processing.

Studies have shown that people differ in their tendency to "favor" one side of the brain over the other. Faced with the task of finding a recipe in a cookbook, for instance, some of us will scan the pages of the book convinced that we can find it quickly, while others prefer to use the index. These two different styles of doing things reflect different brain orientations. The "flipper" displays an instance of right-brain-dominated activity. The "index-scanner" illustrates the linear, left-brain-dominated way of doing things.

Which side do babies prefer? Interestingly, existing evidence suggests that infants have not yet differentiated these learning styles. However, all seem to start with a preference for right-brain kinds of actions and perceptions, preferring curvatures to angular space, responding to rhymes and music, and showing interest in patterns and wholes, not parts or segments of things. These observations point to the ability of the infant brain to perceive, react to, act on, and construct knowledge of the events that impact her mental life. At this very early age, your baby's mind is resilient and ready to make sense of her surroundings.

Other Competencies of Your Newborn

Aside from her motor and sensory abilities, your newborn has some miraculous social abilities. These abilities are designed to endear her to you: she knows her mommy's face and voice and can distinguish them from others, she may be able to imitate your facial expressions, and she can take turns "conversing" with you.

When it comes to a newborn's knowledge of the physical world, you will, once again, be amazed. Your newborn can anticipate where a traveling object is headed; she can trace the outline of a complicated picture, separating one item from another; she can see depth, realizing that there is a drop in the surface of a table or another object; she can detect brightness and movement, and can track a voice by moving her head in the direction of a voice; and she can express surprise at an unexpected event.

Let's look at some ingenious studies that illustrate your newborn's phenomenal abilities.

What Your Newborn Knows About People

Newborns only two to three days old show a preference for their mother's voice and turn their heads in the direction of her voice. This raises the question: Do they learn mother's voice while in the womb, or are they such fast learners that they learn it in the first day or two of life?

DR. SEUSS STORIES

In 1980, DeCasper and Fifer reported a fascinating study that answers this question. Newborns, only two days old, were placed comfortably on their backs with headsets on their ears. A pacifier geared to a tape player was placed in their mouths. When the baby sucked at a certain rate, the tape played her mother's voice reading a Dr. Seuss story. If the baby varied her sucking rate, the tape would continue to play the Dr. Seuss story, only this time it was read by a different woman. Over eighty-five percent of the babies tested adjusted their sucking rate so that they could hear their own mothers' voices. When the experimenters changed the rate at which the baby could hear the mother's voice, the babies quickly adjusted their sucking so they could continue to hear her voice. What's even more impressive is that newborns were able to start a new session where they had left off the previous session! This suggests that they have developed a practical memory—they could remember the previous day's experience!

To find out whether the babies had learned their mothers' voices in those two days after birth or whether they got used to it while they were still in the womb, experimenters recruited the babies' fathers. In 1984, Kolata repeated the experiment, only this time with the father's voice and another man's voice reading the Dr. Suess story. From the moment of birth, babies were handed over to their fathers, who talked to them all the time, sometimes for ten hours at a time, for two to three days. These babies heard no one else except their father. The result: Babies showed no preference for their father's voice. Since the human ear develops well enough to hear at seven months after conception, these fascinating experiments suggest that the fetus learns her mother's voice and develops a preference for it well before she is born.

Face to Face

Newborns know human faces from the moment they are born and prefer them to other objects. In another ingenious experiment, Dr. Robert Fantz of Case Western University studied eye movements of newborns only a few days old. Lying comfortably on their backs, the babies were shown two patterns of the features of a human face (mouth, eyes, nose). One pattern contained all the elements of the face in the proper arrangement. The other pattern, while containing the same mouth, eyes, and nose, was not arranged as a human face. The idea was to see which of the two faces attracted and kept the young children's attention longer. Invariably, newborns preferred the human face to the haphazardly arranged one.

This preference suggests that newborns only a few days old can distinguish one pattern as meaningful while dismissing the other as nonsense. This makes sense; after all, a baby's survival is dependent on her knowledge of the human face, and bonding with her mother or caretaker, relating to her, and interacting with her all depend on knowing a human face.

IMITATING MOMMY OR DADDY

As we mentioned earlier, for years psychologists used to think that newborns couldn't imitate until they were a few months old. More recently, some studies of infant imitation showed that newborns, in fact, have an innate ability to imitate facial expressions.

For example, Andrew Meltzoff conducted many studies on infant imitation. He found that newborns could imitate an adult's facial expressions only hours after birth. Within a few trials they could, for example, stick their tongue out or open their mouths wide just like he did.

The fact newborns prefer human faces and can imitate facial expressions seems to be strong evidence that they know they are human!

CONVERSATIONS...OF SORTS

Only moments after birth, newborns carry on "conversations" by maintaining social interactions with you, if only you give them a chance to take turns. When you talk, your baby will stay still, and when you stop talking, your baby will do something. For example, she might thrash her legs or arms about to interact with you.

What Your Newborn Knows About Things

STRIPES, CONTRASTS

By recording a newborn's eye movements as she looks at a picture, we can tell that she is tracing the outlines of the picture. This ability is critical in telling the difference between an object and its background.

Using the same technique, we know that newborns focus on stripes and color contrasts. This knowledge is important in knowing where one object ends and another begins.

BRIGHTNESS, MOVEMENT, AND TRACKING

Studies have shown that newborns are sensitive to brightness—changing the brightness causes them to squint. We also know that when newborns are only two to three days old, they can detect movement and visually follow a moving object. What's more, newborns can turn their heads in the direction of sound, expecting to see something where the noise is.

SURPRISE, SURPRISE

Another example of how newborns are born knowing certain things is how they respond to surprise. Research shows that babies manifest attention, curiosity, and interest as a natural response to the element of surprise. In addition, PET scans (positron emission tomography), a technique that measures electric activity of the brain, shows that a flurry of brain activity results from an unexpected event.

SEEING IN 3-D

Back when some experts were debating whether newborns can see at all, an incredible experiment carried out in 1960 by Eleanor Gibson of Cornell University showed that babies can not only see, they can perceive depth.

Thirty-six babies between the ages of six and a half and fourteen months were placed in the middle of a transparent table approximately eight feet square. Half of the table was covered with a tablecloth so that the floor was not visible from the tabletop, while the other half was left uncovered so that the floor could be seen easily. Then the entire table was covered with a glass top so that the feel of the surface on both halves would be the same. A baby's mother would stand at the end of the transparent side of the table. The experimenter would then place the baby on top of the table that was covered with the tablecloth. In order to reach his mother, the baby would have to crawl over his half of the table and then over the transparent or "deep" top. Everybody waited to see whether the baby would crawl over to her mother. Most of the babies refused to crawl over the "deep" section of the table. Even when the babies' mothers tried to coax them into crawling toward the transparent side, only three babies tried it. Some, having reached the center, stopped and began crying, presumably wanting to get close to their mothers yet afraid to do so.

Dr. Gibson argued that the ability to perceive depth was not learned, but is inherited. The flaw with Gibson's experiment was that it didn't prove that children hadn't learned depth perception after birth, as all the children in the study were at least six and a half months old. However, later research with even younger children substantiated her claim by using different techniques that did not require the child to crawl. Dr. Gibson herself addressed that concern in her next set of experiments, by using animals that can walk the minute they're born, such as goats. This time, the animals had no chance to learn anything—they either had been born with depth perception or not. Not surprisingly, these animals refused to cross the middle line where the "visual cliff" started.

Conclusion

This is the picture of your newborn's abilities. Far from being a helpless, incompetent, empty receptacle, she comes equipped with some basic sensory and motor skills, plus enough knowledge of people to endear herself to her parents, and she quickly builds on her abilities. She also knows a thing or two about the world of things—such as where one thing ends and another begins, and how to track a moving object. Great as these abilities are, they are not the whole story. What is beneath all of this is a tendency to become a full-fledged human being, to reach her full potential. This tendency is inherent in her. It is what drives her to understand, to make sense of people, events, and things in her life. It is what makes her a meaning maker. Armed with the knowledge of your baby's nature and capacities, we are now ready to take a look at the specific strategies and methods that will help you provide your baby with opportunities for enriching experiences.

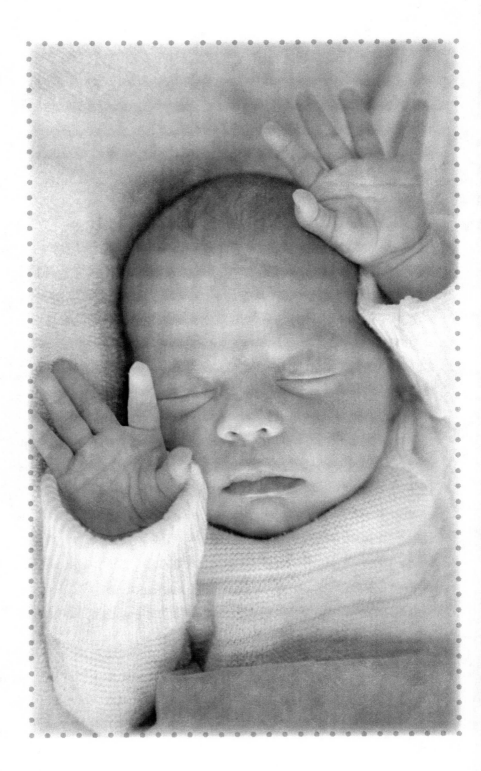

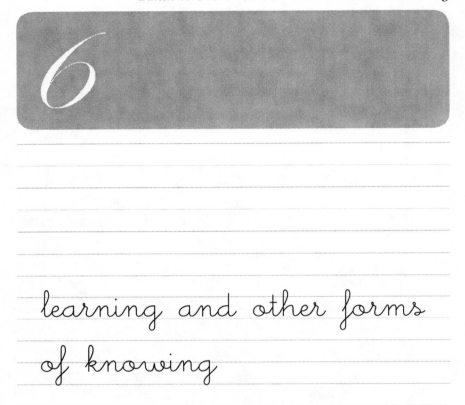

learning and other forms of knowing

How do babies learn? This question is not as simple as it seems. Babies are resilient—they can and do learn in many different ways. They will learn whether we apply the correct methods or not, or even if we don't have a particular method in mind at all.

However, babies do have a natural way of learning about the social and physical world around them. To help them learn, and even more importantly, to help them make sense of their experiences, we need to understand and encourage their way of learning. What is that way?

SIMPLE PERCEPTIONS AND REFLEXES — A GOOD BEGINNING

The natural way that infants develop intelligence and learn is to use the abilities of perception (obviously through all of their senses) as well as their reflexes. Initially, these perceptions and reflexes provide the basis for all of your baby's interactions. For example, when you touch your newborn's mouth with a pacifier, he will start sucking immediately. So far this is only an involuntary response to some form of stimulation—no learning has taken place. By about the third or fourth week, though, a newborn will start sucking at the sight of his bottle. My own twin boys, Koby and Jeremy, would stop crying and begin fidgeting when they saw or heard me shake their formula in the bottle, anticipating mealtime!

This type of learning applies to motor actions as well. For example, when you place your finger in your newborn's hand, he will clutch it firmly and won't let go. But within a month or so, he'll be able to open his hand to let go at will. Moving from the involuntary reflex to exercising control over this simple act is a form of learning.

Infants form knowledge by touching, mouthing, seeing, hearing, smelling, and by acting on the objects or ideas they are trying to understand. For example, your newborn uses his mouth and his hands to explore objects, learning about their taste, texture, and temperature.

In this way the perceptions that he experiences from his senses along with his reflex actions teach the newborn a great deal about the world around him. What's more, these reflex actions and primitive perceptions are the only means by which newborns can experience the world around them.

So, if perception and action are the origins of intelligence, what is the basis for the growth of intelligence? The answer lies in your baby's innate ability and natural tendency to coordinate, or link one action with another—to combine actions with perceptions, and perceptions with other perceptions. Your baby gradually builds a progressively more complicated network of perceptions and actions. The more variable and flexible this network is, the more intelligent your baby's actions become. Think of it this way. If one person knows only one way to perform a task, but another can do the same thing three or four different ways, which one is better off?

For us humans, making sense of the experiences we encounter is a primordial force. It is something we must do because we constantly strive to seek balance in our understanding. "Understanding" means that we try to find equilibrium in our actions and thoughts. Without cognitive equilibrium, our mental life would be uncomfortable, unnatural, and chaotic. Thus in our mental life we like to impose some order, however personal and idiosyncratic that order may be.

When your baby grasps his smooth teething ring, he learns to differentiate it from his rough rattle. Even though these actions are restricted to a few movements and a few primitive perceptions, your baby comes equipped to perceive and act. Developing intellectual skills and learning is as natural for your baby as sucking and grasping. Within a month or so, he will start to link these reflex actions with one another, naturally joining them together to make more elaborate connections. In this way, he expands his knowledge and know-how, extending his ways of knowing. When your baby learns to connect seeing his rattle with grasping it, he can reach for it and grab it. As he coordinates grasping with sucking, he can easily bring the rattle to his mouth. This is an action that, only a month ago, he was unable to carry out. Thus, it is through coordination of actions that babies grow in intelligence. Such coordination results in new learning and more sophisticated ways of knowing.

Factors in Intellectual Development

For decades, child development specialists have pondered the question of mental development. Thanks largely to Piaget's enormous contributions, we now believe that four major factors explain this intriguing process: maturation, physical experience, social learning, and self-regulation. Let's look at the parts to understand how the whole takes shape.

Maturation

As we have seen, babies come equipped with certain innate abilities, which require no training or education. They are the means of survival, learning, and development. These capacities develop as the nervous system matures. This unfolding process is called maturation.

Experience and opportunities to exercise his skills enable your baby to improve upon and expand those skills to their natural limits. Environment plays a significant role in determining the direction and extent to which inherited capacity will be expressed. As we saw in Chapter 4, the child who is raised in a nurturing environment is likely to develop inherited capacities to their fullest potential, while a child raised in a sterile atmosphere rarely fulfills anticipated growth.

However, the process of each baby's maturation does set some limits on the role played by the environment. If an infant is born brain damaged, for example, no degree of environmental stimulation will alter that child's ultimate growth and development limitations. Obviously, the child can and does benefit from experience, but this limitation cannot be overcome with experience alone.

Most authorities believe that while mental growth cannot be forced, it certainly can be nurtured in the proper setting. The question is, how? Our answer lies in providing a broad variety of stage-appropriate enriching experiences, with a healthy dose of parental love, support, and coaching. Let me emphasize again, however, that if the nurturing experiences offered to children are not appropriate to their level of ability, and if children are not given the opportunity to initiate their own actions and choose their own interests, the experiences will be of little benefit. They may even be detrimental, by creating frustration or boredom.

To determine what types of varied, stage-appropriate experiences are necessary to enhance intellectual development, we divide experience into two areas: physical experience, or experience with things; and social experience, or experience with people.

Physical Experience

What is your baby expected to figure out from playing with a simple toy? Is it possible that his interaction with a toy, a material object, can lead to scientific discovery as well as logical development? The answer might surprise you.

BABY SCIENCE

A baby pushing a ball, shaking a rattle, pulling a toy, banging on the table, or dropping a spoon to the floor is learning about things and how they interact with other things. Such encounters with the physical world help your baby to discover the properties of things–what they are like.

Your baby starts by discovering the features of the things that he can touch, see, taste, hear, and smell. Gradually he builds a body of knowledge about material things and how they influence one another as they act upon one another. For instance, when your baby pounds a plastic drinking glass on his highchair tray, he discovers some properties of the glass: its shape, its transparency, the noise it makes, its weight, and its texture. He will discover that the plastic glass makes one noise when he pounds it against his plastic highchair tray, and another noise when it is dropped to the tile floor. Even if his early generalizations are not entirely accurate, they are nonetheless very important, and they will be refined, tested, and revised as time goes on.

In this way, your baby builds knowledge of things. By acting on things and interacting with them, he discovers what is already there-the properties of the objects themselves. In a real sense, this is what "the scientist in the crib" means—it is the foundation of physical science.

Ideally your baby should interact with a variety of objects during his first two years. That is when an appreciation of the world of science is being set. I use "science" here in its most basic and profound sense: the word is rooted in the Latin verb sciere, "to know." If your baby's "experiments" are encouraged, he will not only build a scientific base but also develop an inquisitive attitude toward science in general. This knowledge, and especially his attitude toward learning, will eventually have a great impact when he enters school.

BABY LOGIC

You may be surprised to learn that even your child's logic is constructed out of these physical experiences. How can a child form logical concepts by playing with physical objects?

A vital aspect of interactions with material things involves building knowledge of how to interact with these material objects. When your baby plays with material things, he invents ways of acting on them: how to hold a rattle, how to shake it, how to get it to make a certain noise, how to pick it up, and how to release it. This is what we call know-how.

Suppose you hand your baby a rattle through the slats of his crib, intentionally positioning it so that it is perpendicular to the slats. As he grasps the rattle, it remains pressed against the slats. No matter how hard he pulls, he cannot draw the rattle into the crib because it is stuck against two of the slats. Without hesitation your baby turns the rattle so that it, like the slats, is positioned vertically. Now, he easily pulls it into the crib.

This kind of action is fundamentally different from discovering the properties of the rattle itself. Clearly, it is intelligently planned; it shows great insight. Your baby had to invent a solution to the problem he faced. He had to understand something about his own actions, as opposed to discovering a property of the object itself. What a marvel! This is a preliminary form of reflecting, leading—in time—to thinking about one's own thinking.

Such action is intelligent because it is logical. Essentially, it is as though your baby goes through a reasoning process: "If I pull it this way, it gets stuck; I'll just turn it another way so it will slip through these bars." Of course babies don't reason through such dilemmas like adults do. However, a baby's logic, which is initially on an action level only, eventually leads to the reasoning that approximates logic as we know it.

Consider also the problem of categorization. If I were to ask you to think about areas of a supermarket, you would probably think of the produce department, the meat department, the bakery, the international foods section, and so on. What you've done is to group things according to a certain category. Incredibly, babies also group things along certain features. When your baby can tell the difference between your face and somebody else's, or between the dog and the cat, he is grouping things. When your toddler puts all the horses over here and all the trucks over there, he is classifying items into categories. This act of classification is essentially a logical operation. Your baby must invent a class of objects and then place examples of that object into its class. He builds a "logical" system that he constantly revises.

So, by playing with things, your baby builds two types of knowledge: (1) He discovers properties of the things themselves, and (2) he invents ways of dealing with them. Discovery is finding out about the things themselves; invention is about finding out about one's own abilities. Discovery is a scientific process; invention is a reflective process. Discovery is the means for building scientific knowledge; invention is the means of building logical know-how.

Learning About People and Their Conventions

Experience with objects, otherwise known as physical experience, explains a great deal of what we know and how we come to know it. But how does your baby learn about daily routines such as feeding, bathing, cuddling, and playing? What about learning to wave bye-bye or to respond to his name? Does your baby need to discover or invent these things? Of course not. His name is not a scientific fact that needs to be discovered or a logical truth that needs to be reinvented. It is a made-up label. Waving bye-bye is equally arbitrary. It's as arbitrary as stopping at a red light and going on a green light. These are mere conventions people have developed for their convenience, and these customs make up what is known as conventional knowledge. Conventional knowledge is learned through a process of repetition. It is here that rewarding your child for making a correct response is relevant.

If you encourage your baby to wave bye-bye and he so much as comes close to making the right gesture, you obviously would shower him with smiles, hugs, and words of praise. Chances are that he will repeat this gesture the next time he is encouraged to say bye-bye. In this way, he learns to wave bye-bye. It just takes trial and error plus a form of reinforcement or reward.

These skills all come from a single source: social learning or, more precisely, social transmission. Socially transmitted knowledge comes from people. It has been developed by the culture of the baby and is transmitted to the baby by the people around him. People in general, and parents in particular, directly teach the baby the things that make up his language, eating habits, values, taboos, folklore, rhymes, songs, and stories.

Cultures have invented methods for creating, accumulating, and transmitting artifacts, values, and social rules and conventions. Children learn this type of knowledge by observing, trying and failing, trying and succeeding, repeating, and receiving encouragement.

Through channels of their culture (art, music, language, and education), children assimilate a great deal of socially "convented" knowledge, to coin a word, which forms the foundation for them to learn and master their own culture.

Self-Regulation

To have the seeds of maturation is one thing, but how do those seeds know what to do—how does a tomato seed know how to become a tomato and not a melon? To extend this metaphor, is it simply sunlight, water, and nutrients in the soil that tell a seed what to become, or is there an internal force that guides the seed to be what it is supposed to be by balancing the proper amounts of light, water, and nutrients? Of course there must be some internal ingredient, because if sunlight, water, and good soil were all one needed to grow a plant, then we might bury a toothpick and expect it to grow!

We are also programmed in the same biological way-we have an internal force that puts together our maturational abilities with our physical experience and social learning to make sense of it all. The interesting thing about this process is that it never stops. At every point in our development, this ongoing force is at work, pushing development to its fullest potential. As I said earlier, children are born with abilities that enable them to survive and learn. That, I suppose, is now self-evident. What is not so evident is a newborn's inborn tendency to put these abilities to use in an effort to understand the buzzing world of objects, people, and their interaction.

When my daughter Beth was about two years old, she called a swimming pool "foo na na." (At least she got the number of syllables right!) One day, we took her on vacation to Ocean City, Maryland, where she saw the ocean for the very first time. "Big foo na na!" she exclaimed joyfully. Beth somehow had to deal with a new object of knowledge (ocean). Her regulating mechanism told her not to get confused: "You already know something like this (swimming pool); let's relate this new bit of knowledge to what you already know." Simple. But had she ignored this opportunity for learning a new concept, she would not have moved in the direction of higher forms of knowing. The regulating system insists that the knower somehow grapple with a new concept in an effort to achieve a higher level of knowledge.

There will be times when this sort of easy regulating is challenged. For example, we might have told Beth, "This is not a swimming pool. This is an ocean." Chances are that, at that stage of her development, she would have ignored our remark completely and maintained that it was a "big foo na na." At a somewhat later stage, though, the challenge might have had an impact, and she would have been forced to create a difference between swimming pool and ocean.

Your baby's development has a specific direction—toward better ways of knowing. Just as your baby moves from crawling to walking to running, so too do his ways of knowing, or "learning to know," move from simple to complex, from the physical act to the mental image to the symbol, from the here and now to the past and future, from the concrete to the abstract. This movement is toward more and more adult-like thinking.

What explains this movement toward higher and higher levels of functioning? The answer lies in the concept of equilibration, a term that comes from equilibrium or balance.

Equilibrium is a state where things are in balance, but equilibration is an ongoing process, one of continuous mental adjustment in an effort to strike a balance between what your baby already knows and what he is trying to understand.

Think of equilibration as a regulator within your baby that constantly monitors activity in order to avoid confusion with every little bit of knowledge that comes along. Just as a thermostat regulates the heat in your house by registering what the temperature is and adjusting it to what you set it to be, your baby's regulator adjusts what it already knows with what it encounters.

First the regulator tries to relate the object of knowledge to what your baby already knows. If it can, then the old knowledge is revised. If it can't, then it constructs a new category of knowledge. In short, the regulator's role is to fit new knowledge into your baby's developing concept of the world, either by relating it to what is known or by marking it as something new.

Our understanding all of this can be of great benefit to our children. By being aware of how your baby reacts to a correction, you can expedite this self-regulation process. There are two things to look for.

If your baby is corrected yet maintains his old way of doing things, he probably needs more time to play with the concept before he is ready to change—just as Beth might have ignored the pool/ocean correction. That would have been a sign that she needed more time and experience with the old concept she had created. We might have shown her a small plastic wading pool (which she had), then a neighborhood-sized pool (like the one at the hotel), to focus her attention on the difference between her pool and the swimming pool. However, while you can offer examples to guide this process, it is very important to let your baby process such distinctions at his own pace. Children require their own amount of time to assimilate new concepts fully before they are ready to create new concepts for themselves.

On the other hand, when your correction creates a puzzle, a surprise for your child, then he is ready to learn the new concept. When your baby isn't ready for a new concept, it is as if your correction doesn't even register. However, if your correction triggers a puzzled look or evokes a question, then you can be certain it has not only registered but has created a "disturbance," a mental disequilibrium. Aha! Now your child needs more experience with the new concept. For instance, to distinguish the ocean from a swimming pool, Beth needed to discover that the ocean has waves, that its water is salty, its bottom is sandy, and so on. Playing at the beach reinforced her ability to distinguish between the two objects of knowledge, which helped her to construct the new concept. Like all other forms of learning, conceptual learning needs practice. After your baby has had enough practice (in a casual, playful setting) and has mastered the concept, he will be ready to move on to another related concept.

Equilibration is an important factor in understanding and facilitating your baby's intellectual development. But remember, maturation, physical experience, and social experience are equally indispensable. After all, intellectual growth is a very complex process. One factor alone cannot explain it, for it is the product of the interaction among the four parts.

It is fascinating to consider the limitless possibilities of your baby's intellectual growth. All of this can be enhanced by your understanding, input, and encouragement—not to mention your delight at being an integral part of the process.

To understand the intricacies of intellectual development and to gain a full appreciation of the task of enriching your baby's mind, let us take a look at the concept of developmental stages.

Mental Development Progresses in Phases and Stages

Contrary to popular belief, intellectual development is not a linear progression ascending smoothly upward. In reality, mental development between birth and adulthood can best be described as a spiral with four major turns, each constituting a distinct way of knowing—a phase. The four major phases are: Sensorimotor Intelligence (birth through two years); Preoperational Thought (two through seven or eight years); Concrete Operational Thought (seven or eight through twelve through fourteen); and Formal Operational Thought (twelve or fourteen on). This book is concerned with only the first phase of intellectual development, the sensorimotor phase.

The Sensorimotor Phase

In the sensorimotor phase, your baby's ways of knowing are limited to the senses and physical action. A form of practical intelligence, sensorimotor knowing enables babies to adapt to their immediate environment. However, the sensorimotor baby lacks a mature symbolic system, and is simply stuck in the here and now. Unable to make words and images stand for real objects and events, he can understand only what he can perceive and what he can do. This is particularly true during the first year of life.

During the second year, and certainly by the end of that year, your baby begins to construct a representational system, displaying the ability to mentally represent objects and events in their absence. This includes the use of simple words and phrases to speak of things not perceived (mostly wants and needs), images of absent objects (understanding

the fact that disappearing objects do not cease to exist altogether), and abbreviated movements (using gestures and
hand motions to convey ideas).

By the end of the second year, your baby's intellect starts
to soar. As his symbolic system develops, it enables your
baby to image something, imitate people, and talk about an
absent event. A new and wonderful world of knowing opens
up with the onset of the symbolic system. Now your child
can offer reasons for things, although, by our standards,
the rationale or intuition of a two-year-old is often entirely
wrong! This process is a gradual one, showing that the
appearance of mental abilities doesn't sprout overnight,
but evolves over time and with experience.

Each phase, period, or stage builds on the preceding one,
advancing your baby to a new and more elaborate, flexible,
and adult-like way of thinking. A cognitive stage, then, con-
stitutes a manner of knowing—a way of understanding.

Within the sensorimotor phase, between birth and roughly
the end of the second year, babies go through six specific
stages. Think of the six sensorimotor stages of infancy as
an upward spiral with six turns, each turn a little larger than
the one below (preceding) it. Each stage becomes a foundation for building the next.

Stages are sequential, following one another in an orderly
manner. Each of us passes through the four periods I outlined
earlier (as well as the stages within them) without skipping.
Your baby must attain one stage before going on to the

next, and this progression of attainments cannot be altered. Children the world over undergo stages in the same order, although the speed with which they complete them may vary.

STAGE I

In Stage I (birth through the first month), your baby is restricted to the use of reflex actions. Because his knowledge system is tied to such ways of knowing as grasping and sucking, your baby knows things only if they trigger these reflex actions.

Thus objects or events in your baby's surroundings set off, or trigger, the appropriate reflex without your baby forming a conscious intention to act. In addition, your baby cannot yet put these reflexes together to form a single coherent action. Each reflex functions independently. So while your baby can grasp a rattle placed in his hand, or suck on a rattle, he can't easily pick it up and bring it to his mouth himself—yet.

STAGE II

When your baby is able to coordinate one reflex action with another, creating new action patterns that are more organized, elaborate, and whole we can say that he has reached Stage II. Your baby can now acquire new patterns of behavior by integrating one act with another, then undoing the integration and combining actions in an entirely new way. This ability to integrate and differentiate actions enables your baby to construct new ways of doing things, new ways of organizing and adapting to reality. This expands the realm of learning, enabling your baby to start "playing" and "imitating."

Coordinating hand and mouth, following objects with his eyes, turning his head in the direction of sound, producing sounds or vocalizing, imitating sounds he could already produce, and other elements of early play are all examples of the cognitive abilities your baby displays in Stage II. Your baby's actions are oriented toward himself and are at first produced unintentionally. Your baby can now repeat actions he has already performed, and every time he repeats them, new objects are incorporated into his scheme of the action.

STAGE III

The ability to exercise skills by manipulating the external world of objects is the distinguishing characteristic of the Stage III baby (four to eight months). Your baby can now reproduce an event that he had caused accidentally and found interesting. For example, your baby may notice that the mobile suspended above him moves when he thrashes his legs around in his crib. He'll thrash around again to try to make the mobile move. If he succeeds, he will repeat the process again and again. Your baby actually enjoys repeating the patterns of behavior he learns!

His behavior is exciting for two reasons. First, it is directed toward an object outside his own body; second, the action is repeated. If your baby perceives a relationship between his act and the resulting event, he must be forming a primitive but practical understanding of cause and effect, or the means-ends principle. Doing this, he has learned, produces that.

STAGE IV

After the rapid learning of Stage III, in Stage IV (eight to twelve months) your baby consolidates his past learning and applies it to new situations. In this stage your baby perfects a number of major attainments, beginning with the concept of means-ends relations. Your baby now intentionally selects means to accomplish pre-established goals, and he develops his concept of space and time more fully. On a practical level only, your baby understands concepts such as "in," "out," "behind," and "through." This helps your baby understand the concept of the permanence of objects. In the previous stage, your baby could only search for a disappearing object visually; now, he begins to search manually! This important development shows your baby's advancement in understanding that objects can go out of sight without totally vanishing from the world.

Peek-a-boo becomes intensely interesting to your baby in this stage. Imitating has progressed to the point where your baby can reproduce an action that involves parts of his body he cannot see. He can also anticipate events that are usually preceded by other familiar events. When the usual sequence is changed, he will express surprise.

STAGE V

Now a toddler, the Stage V child (twelve to eighteen months) can experiment and solve problems, initially through trial and error, but later on, quite efficiently. He intentionally and systematically varies an action to discover how changes in his actions affect the outcome. He understands that not only he but other people and objects can cause things to happen. He has constructed some idea of time, of space, and of how objects fit in and out of things. He knows that if an object has been moved from one hiding place to another, he'll find it by looking where it was last seen. And he can imitate novel acts—acts that he has not imitated before.

Because your baby is beginning to develop the capacity to represent objects and events mentally through images, words, and abbreviated actions, he is freed from a knowledge system that was restricted to what he could touch, see, hear, smell, and taste. Now he is able to know things by imaging them. Stage V is the beginning of the end of sensorimotor intelligence. Over the next year or so, your baby's symbolic system will have evolved to the point where an entirely new phase of knowing becomes possible.

Most children say their first words in this stage of development. While there is a great variation in the rate of development from child to child, if your baby does not begin to speak by the end of Stage V, it may be sign of an underlying problem. If this is the case, you should consult your pediatrician for a professional evaluation.

STAGE VI

In this last stage of the sensorimotoric period (eighteen to twenty-four months), your baby's symbolic system is so well developed he can solve problems without resorting to the trial-and-error experimentation he showed in Stage V. Now he can run through the solution to a problem mentally and then solve it. Stage VI is a transition period, one that, upon its completion, will hurl the child into the world of thought. Parents delight in witnessing the phenomenon of insight: when confronted with a problem, the child shows little or no physical groping before hitting on a solution. As this period ends, a new mode of mental activity characterized by a magical, intuitive, and egocentric kind of thought begins— the thought of the preschooler.

Lessons From Infant Day Care

When it comes to general guidelines for enriching babies' and young children's intellects, we can learn a great deal from professional infant day-care educators, who design enriching environments to promote beneficial activities.

Following are some suggestions professionals in this field have for caregivers and teachers in these settings. In many ways, these tips are appropriate to parents, as well.

- Accept that individual children will differ in temperament and approach; do not expect one child to react to the same challenge in the same way another might.
- Offer toys that are appropriate to age and stage.
- Avoid interruptions and corrections.
- Smile; make eye contact.

- Show delight when the child succeeds.

- Don't give complicated instructions. Make sure the language you use is comprehensible.

- Be prepared for new variations on uses of playthings that you (or others) may not have anticipated. Just be sure to keep baby's safety in mind at all times.

- Remember that the child's showing puzzlement at a new concept is a good sign.

- Help the child master activities by encouraging repetition. Bear in mind where the child has given up in the past with a certain plaything. Next time, help the child resume at that point.

- When appropriate, direct the child to a parallel but simpler activity.

- Demonstrate by playing with the toy yourself first.

- Provide the next level of challenge with a toy or concept before the child becomes bored with it. (This may take some practice on your part to learn exactly when the restlessness is likely to set in.)

- Encourage new associations and combinations.

- Encourage cooperation with others by showing delight at instances of sharing and playing with companions.

- Be available to share discoveries, consult on problems, and offer support—but don't do the playing for the child.

The best approach is to maintain a presence such that the baby knows you are there to appeal to if necessary.

- Listen to the actual words and to the more subtle types of communication, such as glances and body language.

- Avoid showing discouragement or impatience at instances of what you may consider "failure" at a given task. (Doing so may actually pose developmental obstacles for the child.) Instead, put the accent on positive reinforce ment and unconditional affection.

- Highlight those activities, friendships, and playthings that have been demonstrated to be of interest to the child. (Why focus on that for which the child has demonstrated he has no interest?)

The next section of this book provides in-depth discussions of each stage, including suggestions for activities and toys that are appropriate for your baby at each stage. Please remember that these activities are not a "prescription" for building a "better" baby. Rather, they are guidelines for making the most of each stage of your baby's development. Whether you try them all, or focus only on a select few, let your baby's interests guide you. Now let us explore the path your baby will follow through the stages of sensorimotor intelligence.

7

stage 1:
birth to one month

We all realize how dependent our newborn babies are on us. They depend on us for food, clothing, caring, love, and learning. In fact, human infants, of all the other animals, are the most dependent upon their caretakers, and they remain dependent for the longest period of time. Yet despite this, as we have already seen, our babies are well equipped to adapt to and interact with their surroundings from the instant of birth.

However, many parents don't have the slightest idea of what their newborns are capable of. For the most part, parents see their newborns as bundles of joy who need to be fed and diapered, but not much else.

Unfortunately, the common misconceptions we have long accepted create a double tragedy. First, a newborn's parents have such low expectations of their baby's capabilities that they simply don't bother to offer any special enrichment. Consequently, they miss out on the joys that come with observing and aiding their child's earliest development. Second, as a result of her parents' low expectations and their failure to provide more than mere "bodily" attention, the baby misses the significant early enrichment that can mean so much intellectually later in life.

Your baby's effort to make meaning of the world begins at birth. Realizing how she does it will bring a new joy to your attitude about early parenting.

What a Newborn Knows

In Chapter 5 we discussed what research has taught us about a newborn's sensory, motor, social, and language skills. Before we discuss effective Stage I enrichment, let's review the basic points.

SENSORY ABILITIES

From birth, and certainly by the first week of life, your baby has a fully developed sense of taste and smell.

Your baby's eyes focus best on objects about seven to eight inches away directly in front of her face.

When trying to attract your baby's attention with visual cues, be certain that you stay within the seven-to-eight inch range. Your baby can discern patterns, preferring contrast, contour, and curvy lines over geometric, angular shapes. Use bold print objects with great contrast—black and white is an excellent choice. However, babies are most interested in human faces, so give her lots of opportunities to look at yours!

However briefly, babies pay attention to the location of sound. They respond to all elements of sound, including pitch, volume, timbre, and rhythm. They can even stop sucking to pay attention to something else. After prolonged exposure, babies stop reacting to irritating stimuli. This helps them shut out disturbing sights and sounds.

MOTOR SKILLS

In addition to sensory powers, your baby is born with a working motor system, which is the basis of much of her future learning and development. At the heart of this system is a set of survival and learning reflexes. These reflexes include: crying, vocalizing, sneezing, coughing, sucking, eye movements (blinking, focusing, tracking), grasping, and swallowing. Objects or events in your baby's surroundings trigger these actions. If, for example, you stroke your baby's cheek or the area near her mouth with your hand, her head turns and her tongue moves toward your hand. Once she finds your hand, she begins sucking. Or, if you shine a small light into her eyes, or clap your hands in front of her face, she will close her eyes tightly.

SELECTED REFLEXES OF NEWBORNS

REFLEX	DESCRIPTION
Automatic Walking	Walking movements with feet when supported to a standing position
Babinski	Toes spread out when soles of feet are stimulated.
Blinking	Eyes closes tightly when bridge of her nose gently tapped.
Crawling	Turns head to side, lifts self with arms, makes crawling motion when placed on tummy.
Grasping	Grasps very firmly at finger placed in palm.
Moro	Head drops back, arms fly out to the side, and fingers extend when sudden noise or contact is made, or when newborn is "dropped" in the air a few inches and held again.
Rooting	Turns in the direction of the stimulus when cheeks are stroked.
Sucking	Sucking begins when baby's lips or mouth area are stroked.

At birth, your baby's reflexes are mostly isolated, under-developed, and clumsy. For the first month or so, they seem to function independently of one another. For instance, the grasping reflex is not connected with sucking, and your baby does not seem to have any awareness of stimulus events that trigger her reflexes.

In addition, these reflex actions operate in a mechanical way. Thus, objects and events in your baby's surroundings set off the appropriate reflex without your baby forming a conscious intention to act. Gradually your baby will begin to coordinate various reflexes with one another, such as when she grasps a rattle and gums it. However, this type of coor-dination is not expected until the end of the first month of life, and it signals the beginning of a new stage of intellect, which we refer to as Stage II. But don't expect to see all of these reflexes coordinated in the second month.

Of course, not all reflex actions play an important role in intellectual development. While grasping, sucking, and eye movements are the stuff from which intelligence is built, sneezing and coughing do absolutely nothing to promote mental growth.

Now: how does a baby gain knowledge through these re-flex actions and elementary sensory perceptions?

Sensorimotor Intelligence

In the first month of life, your baby uses her reflex actions. Because her knowledge system is restricted to such ways of knowing as grasping, sucking, and eye movements, things are known only if they trigger these reflex actions. If an object cannot be grasped, placed in the mouth, or looked at closely, then from your baby's point of view it may as well not exist.

It bears repeating that at this stage your baby's knowledge is not represented mentally. Rather, it is supremely functional. In the first month of life, the ability to keep an image of things in one's mind has not yet been developed. (A possible limited exception is those children who have been shown to imitate facial expressions, as we mentioned in Chapter 5, but not all newborns demonstrate this ability.) Your baby's knowledge is limited to reflexes and primitive perceptions as they interact with the to-be-known object. In Stage I, your baby's major preoccupation during her waking alert hours (about one hour in every ten) is exercising her reflexes and perceptions. Babies have an intrinsic desire to exercise the skills they develop. Mastery of skills seems to be an integral part of their mental lives, and their innate desire to know more invariably leads them to coordinate one skill with another.

The Stage I enrichment objective is to refine your baby's reflex actions and to ready them for the next step in mental development—coordinating reflex actions with one another.

In an earlier chapter, I pointed out that putting skills together, taking them apart, and then reintegrating them in new combinations is the key to understanding mental growth. But your baby doesn't exist in a vacuum; her actions always involve objects, events, and people. As your baby interacts with the objects around her, she begins to make sense of them.

For example: as your baby holds your finger, she is applying the grasping function to it. In doing so, she is discovering properties of your finger, such as its size, warmth, and feel, thereby learning about your finger as an object, a "content area." Applying her reflex actions to a wide variety of objects and events (content areas) helps your baby construct knowledge.

Piaget, following the insights of the renowned philosopher Emanuel Kant, proposed that the most important content areas for the development of the human mind were object, time, space, and causality. By seeing how babies apply their skills to these content areas, we can deduce how they construct knowledge from them.

The Object Concept

In its mature form, the object concept refers to the knowledge that an object will continue to exist even though we cannot directly sense it. For instance, I don't see my car right now, yet I know (or believe) that it exists. I don't have to perceive it to know that it is still in my garage.

Infants are not born with this ability. They must construct it bit by bit. Normally, it takes approximately ten months for newborns to begin searching manually for a hidden object, a good indication that they know the object continues to exist even though they can't see it or feel it.

During the first month of life, babies show no sign whatsoever of this concept, and, what's more, they cannot differentiate themselves from other objects in their surroundings. Because this differentiation is not yet made, Stage I babies cannot begin to construct the concept of the permanence of objects. Similarly, in the first month of life, infants' concepts of time, space, and causality are nonexistent as well.

Enrichment: The Social Scene

As your baby matures and gains experience, she will master her limited system of reflexes and perceptions to develop new, coordinated abilities. How can you help enhance this natural process?

First, be aware of differences between her abilities and yours. For instance, your baby's eyes are about half the size of yours. Because they are not fully developed, she can only focus on objects that are seven to eight inches away from her face.

Even when your baby does see an object, she will have difficulty making sense of it. Your baby transmits visual images to her brain relatively slowly, and she needs time to process the information she gathers. The result is that she responds more slowly to a visual stimulus than you do. While this appears limiting, it may in fact be a remarkable built-in mechanism allowing your baby to focus on objects that are useful to her (such as your fact, your hands, or the nipple) and filter out distractions.

Later, between four and six months of age, when there is a need to reach for objects, your baby's eyes will converge on objects that are farther away. Her visual system, as well as her ability to coordinate her vision with her hand and arm movements, will also have matured by that time.

Second, respect the delicate balance between enrichment and your baby's emotional, physical, and mental state. To take full advantage of an enrichment opportunity, your baby should be calm, alert, and content. Offer just enough interaction to create interest while avoiding overstimulation, which could lead to confusion. If you overstimulate her at this age, your baby will turn you off by falling asleep!

Remember, our babies learn best when guided by their own interests. Your love and caring create the optimal environment for learning in a spirit of fun. Also, let's remember that whatever we do must be done with your baby's safety in mind.

SAFETY CHECK

As you begin, keep in mind that your baby's head is large compared to the rest of her body, and her neck muscles are weak. When you pick her up, carry her, or prop her up, make sure you provide adequate support for her back, neck, and head.

Some of the following exercises call for placing your baby on her stomach. Your baby should always be placed on a comfortable, firm surface. Fluffy bedding, waterbeds, and beanbag chairs can all pose suffocation hazards to young children; babies should not be placed on these items in any position. If your baby should fall asleep on her tummy during an exercise, gently turn her over. Stomach sleeping has been associated with an increased risk of SIDS.

Finally, though your baby will probably be doing more looking and listening than touching at this stage, the toys and objects she does handle should be made of non-breakable, nontoxic materials. Make sure that there are no small pieces that can come off and pose choking hazards.

Creating an Enriching Environment

Bold contrastingly sharp patterns for baby to look at and later play with.

Make a large banner using a solid color of felt or flannel. Cut out varying shapes and patterns from other colored swatches of material. Attach Velcro to the backs of these pieces and place them on the solid banner to create an interesting pattern or picture. Remember, this is the time to emphasize contours, patterns, and contrasts. Change the colors, shapes, and designs as your baby grows older. At around sixteen or seventeen months, your baby will be ready to help you place the pieces on your banner. Eventually, the banner can be used to help teach your child shapes and colors. During the early months of life, hang this banner approximately two feet from your baby's crib so that she can see it clearly.

Bold, contrastingly sharp patterns for baby's crib sheet.

As we know, babies prefer to look at human faces. So why not use crib sheets, blankets, and bumpers with large patterns of faces printed on them? Even simple, cartoon-type drawings will do just fine.

A crib bumper with good color contrasts.

This is important for enriching eye movements, as well as for safety and protection.

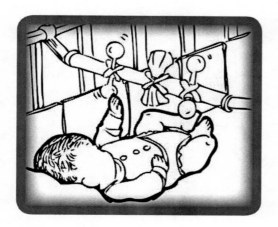

A ribbon or elastic tied across the crib rails to which various objects and small toys are tied.

Tie a ribbon or elastic across the crib rails about seven to eight inches from your baby, tying various objects and small toys to it, such as a light rattle, a swatch of colorful cloth, a plastic spoon, or a small stuffed toy. Your baby will delight in looking at these objects as they move about. For visual variety, change the position of the toys and objects, and periodically change them altogether. fine.

Be certain all objects are firmly attached to the elastic and always choose soft, safe objects (light enough so that if they accidentally fall, your baby won't get hurt, but large enough that they can't be swallowed). Always supervise your baby during this activity and remove the elastic promptly when playtime is over, as it can be dangerous to leave items tied across the crib, especially as your baby becomes older and more mobile.

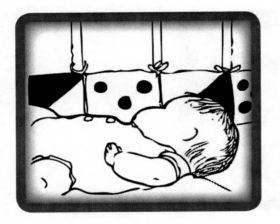

A black and white blanket for playtime

Your baby's attention is drawn to contrasting hues. A black and white checkerboard blanket containing twelve to sixteen squares with different shapes and figures in each square will be a source of interest for your baby. Use this blanket when you put your baby on her stomach for a few minutes. This will help strengthen her back and neck muscles.

A mobile.

A simple mobile is best at this stage. Decorate a paper plate with a black and white spiral design, then suspend it from the ceiling with a ribbon.

Whether you buy or make your own mobile, remember that a mobile should have the baby in mind, not the adult. Your baby will be on her back most of the time, looking at the mobile from below. Thus, as well as emphasizing visual stimuli interesting to your baby (boldness, contrast, and contour), your mobile should look at least as interesting from the bottom as it does from the side.

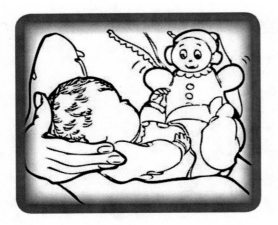

A hand puppet.

Since human faces are so interest-ing to babies, make or buy a puppet that has human features. You can make the puppet move, talk, or sing to your baby.

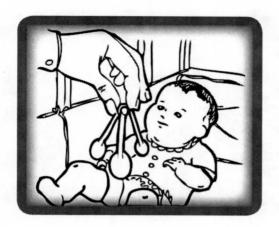

Common kitchen objects, such as plastic measuring spoons or cups.

Try putting on a variety show. Simply show these common objects to your baby for a minute or two while you talk to her. Soon, after daily repetitions of this process, your baby will start reaching for familiar objects. This will be your signal that she has entered Stage II.

Help your baby do "sit-ups".

Place a finger into each of your baby's hands and gently pull
her into a sitting position. You will notice that her arms and
legs move when she gets excited and that when you place
your finger in the palm of her hand, she will tend to grasp
it. How strong her grip is during the first month of life! To
nurture this reflex action, place soft objects and toys into
her hand: a hand towel, a large wooden spoon, a rattle,
or a large plastic ring. Any of these objects, which provide
a variety of shapes, textures, and colors, can be used to
encourage the grasping and sucking reflexes.

Talk, sing, play soft music.

Toward the end of your baby's first month of life, she makes tiny throaty sounds and responds to human voices. But just because she can't talk back or sing along does not mean that you shouldn't talk or sing to her frequently.

When you talk or sing to your baby, you are participating in the earliest beginnings of language development and helping her increase her own vocal activity. Since your baby's sense of hearing is finely tuned, use your voice to soothe her when she is fussy. It should go without saying that addressing your baby by name is an excellent idea at this stage, and indeed, during the other five stages as well.

Touch your baby's cheeks.

Touch your baby's cheeks. At first she will respond wildly when either cheek is touched. Later she will turn toward whichever cheek is being stimulated. Does she respond differently when her cheek is rubbed rather than stroked gently? Stroking stimulates the rooting reflex, triggering the drive to eat. Touch her cheek with the satin edge of a blanket, then with your skin, a sweater, a rattle, a rubber ball. Your skin may set off the most rooting, as your baby begins to associate skin with the nourishment and affection that often follow a touch. This enhances your baby's early development of accommodation—fitting her behavior to the object she is in contact with.

Touch your baby's lips.

Gently touch your fingers to your baby's lips. Does she start to suck? As a variation, try brushing her lips with a soft toy. Your baby is developing the ability to discriminate between nipples, fingers, toys, and so on. This activity also helps your baby to gain control over the sucking reflex. In Stage II, your baby may start to lick rather than suck. This is a progression from simply sucking.

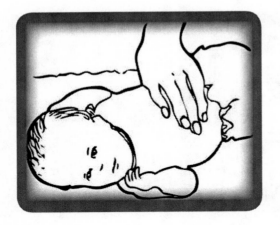

Massage your baby on a daily basis.

I highly recommend massaging your baby on a daily basis. This stimulates your baby's muscles and makes them more responsive. Massaging is not just a wonderful way to awaken your baby's muscles when she wakes up from a nap; it is also a great bonding activity. Holding, touching, hugging, and massaging are as essential to your baby's mind as they are to her emotional development. Talk, sing, or play music as you massage her!

Language Skills

As I discussed in Chapter 3, I consider reading to young babies to be an overrated activity. However, promoting early language development is very important. What should we expect during the first two years of life and what should our role be?

The very word infant derives from the Latin infans, which means "without language." So why bother with a discussion of language here? The answer is straightforward: while babies can't use language to express themselves, they nevertheless are forming the foundation for doing so.

In the first year of her life, your baby will vocalize, uttering sounds that are the precursors of language. These vocalizations are your baby's announcement that she can produce speech sounds.

Four distinct types of vocalizations have been observed in all normal babies, regardless of the culture in which they are raised. Universally, babies are first capable of crying and grunting. Crying is usually associated with some sort of arousal or need state such as hunger, thirst, or pain.

Near the end of the third month, your baby begins to produce utterances best described as cooing. She takes up the prolonged vowel-like sounds with great enthusiasm; we might guess now that your baby is trying to communicate.

By about the sixth month of life, your baby enters a third stage of language development, babbling. Babbling differs from cooing in that it involves a combination of vowel and consonant sounds producing utterances like "mamamama." Interestingly, we still cannot distinguish between an American baby and a Chinese baby at this stage strictly based on their babbling. Babies the world over babble much the same way. Soon pitch variation begins to appear in the babbling.

Not until the fourth stage, with the production of patterned speech, do children actually begin to tune into speech sounds and patterns in their native language, the language being spoken around them.

By their first birthday, babies use intonation to indicate commands and, later on, to indicate questions using single words. At this point, you might notice your child's gradual approximations approaching recognizable words: from dodi to goggie to doggie. Such meaningful words don't usually appear until the first birthday.

Research has shown that the word mama is the first word that most babies utter. Research has also shown that babies' first words have to do with one of three categories: animals, food, and toys. They are also related to desires, perceptions, and emotions. Action words such as eat are among the first to appear. These action words first describe only the baby's action; later, the same word may be used to describe someone else's actions. Bear in mind that the sequence of events is the important thing; variations in the age at which these milestones appear are completely normal.

For the first six months or so your contribution to language development should consist primarily of exchanges of simple expressions and your own simple phrases as you interact with the baby. Be sure to take turns even in your earliest "conversations" with your baby. Start with a smile as you look into her eyes and say a few words. Wait. Give her a chance to react. This waiting time is essential; the gap establishes a chance for your baby to participate. You may only get a stare, or perhaps a cooing sound. Now it's your turn. The idea is to offer an occasion for taking turns.

As you interact with your baby, you can start introducing her to concepts and words to describe her new experiences. For example:

- When you pick up, roll over, or feed your baby, use descriptive words to characterize the way things might feel to her.

- Point out variations in temperatures, textures, etc.

Give your baby plenty of opportunities to hear adults and children talk. Listening to human speech is a natural and necessary part of learning language.

During the second six months, you can add other activities and games to your language-development repertoire. Playing games that name body parts, labeling the objects your baby has daily contact with, and taking walks to point out, touch, and see different things are all excellent activities. Toy telephones can also stimulate your baby to "talk" like you do!

Moving On

Stage I babies are capable of surviving and flourishing in a loving, nurturing human environment, even though they are restricted to a few reflexes and primitive perceptions. Your support in helping your baby master these reflexes will help her move smoothly into Stage II, where she begins to put her abilities together.

Remember that all of my suggestions for this stage and the ones that follow are based on certain fundamental understandings: that the joy of parenting starts with an attitude and atmosphere of relaxed warmth, love, and caring; that activities should be enjoyed in a spirit of fun and guided play, when your baby is attentive and in a calm, relaxed state; and that respect for your baby's comfort and safety should never be overlooked.

SUMMARY OF INTELLECTUAL ATTAINMENTS — STAGE 1: BIRTH TO ONE MONTH

- She focuses on objects about eight inches away and prefers to look at human faces, contours, and contrasts.
- She enjoys sounds, especially high-pitched voices and soft music.
- She grasps objects firmly when they are placed in her hand.
- She shuts out overstimulation by falling asleep.
- She turns to face an object touching her cheeks, and sucks on an object touching her mouth.
- She responds to touch.
- She vocalizes by crying and grunting.

Please remember that a stage is defined by the appearance and persistence of certain specific attainments and limitations. Although we speak of age boundaries to each stage, these are only general guidelines of when attainments usually appear. Normal variations in early development mean that every child will pass through these stages at their own speed and in their own way. Age does not determine stage—it is only an approximation of when a given action is expected.

stage 2:

one to four months

When your baby was in his first month of life (Stage I), his knowledge system was limited to objects or situations that triggered simple survival reflex actions. These were independent actions, with no connection to each other. Exercising these reflex actions helped to refine them.

Now that your baby is one month old, you will notice him begin to coordinate and organize separate reflex actions, and his new action patterns will become more elaborate. Stage II ushers in the possibility of acquiring new patterns of behavior by interacting with the environment. Your baby has a newly developed ability to learn and acquire his first habits. This is body-oriented learning.

During Stage I, for example, sucking was a purely reflexive action designed to nourish your baby. In Stage II your baby sucks not only for nourishment, but for pleasure and exploration as well. He learns to suck his thumb, thereby differentiating the need (hunger) from the act (sucking). This ability to coordinate one action with another opens up a magnificent new world of learning.

Stage II brings us to the heart of all learning: the continuous process of differentiation and integration; that is, disconnecting actions from one another and putting them together in a different way, a way that was not possible before.

Stage II babies can, for instance, learn to change their grasp of an object according to its shape or to adjust their posture according to the way they are held. These apparently small accommodations are in fact the signposts of profound mental growth. They represent adaptations to one's surroundings—in short, intelligence. Without this process, human learning would be impossible.

Here's an example. In an ingenious experiment, psychologists Kalins and Bruner placed babies only three to four months old in front of a screen and gave them a pacifier device hooked up to a focusing mechanism. If the baby sucked on the pacifier rapidly, a picture on the screen would come into focus. If, on the other hand, the baby stopped sucking, the picture went out of focus. The babies quickly learned to speed up their sucking to focus the picture and, in fact, seemed to derive pleasure from "solving" this little puzzle. When the experimenters later reversed the task so that it was necessary to stop sucking in order to focus the image, the babies learned to do that as well!

PRIMARY CIRCULAR REACTIONS

Your baby will gradually progress from the pure reflexes of Stage I to the kind of intentional action demonstrated in this study. At this stage, your baby's actions are oriented toward himself and are first produced unintentionally. However, once he produces an action, your baby can repeat it. With each repetition, he adds new objects into his scheme of the action.

For example, quite by chance your baby brings his hand to his face and suddenly finds his thumb in his mouth. He repeats the action over and over again until it is well learned and easily repeatable. This type of action, which characterizes Stage II, is called a primary circular reaction—primary because it involves your baby's body, and circular because he can repeat it over and over.

Primary circular reactions show that your baby can extend reflex actions into semi-intentional acts, a profound accomplishment that represents a major advance from the reactions of Stage I. To accomplish the thumb-sucking feat, your baby had to differentiate his hand from his mouth. He now looks at his hand as a separate object. And even though he invented the action by accident, he can repeat it.

Your contribution to this achievement should be to help your baby find his hand again by removing distracting objects. In general, at this stage you should be aware of the importance of repetitive actions involving your baby's own body and encourage them.

Refinements (With a Purpose)

In his first month of life you saw your baby busily refining his innately given reflexes and primitive perceptions. By practicing his reflex actions and his perceptual skills, your baby improved his physical skills. During Stage II your baby performs these skills with even greater refinement. The difference is that he now combines his well-practiced skills to accomplish some practical goal. Refinements involving the mouth, hands, eyes, legs, and body are the main focus at this point.

SAFETY CHECK

As in Stage I, at the beginning of Stage II your baby will probably need plenty of support for his neck and head, as his neck muscles gradually get stronger. By the end of this stage, though, your baby may be rolling over. Be sure that your baby's environment contains only safe toys and objects, and be aware of his increasing range of activity and motion.

MOUTH
Try a few games to encourage refinements related to the mouth area.

Perform a "taste test."
Can your baby tell the difference between certain tastes and temperatures of liquids? Does drooling change when he is given chilled formula or breast milk versus warmed, or cold versus warm water?

Give your baby a variety of textured objects
Let him handle and mouth them. Be sure they are non-toxic and safe, and remember, don't overwhelm your baby; present only one new object at a time. Try wooden spoons, wooden rings, plastic balls, terrycloth, velvet, silky material, or rubber.

HANDS
Even now, your baby enjoys grasping your finger when you place it in his palm. Provide opportunities for exercising this action.

"Test" your baby's grip

Place your finger in the palm of his hand and watch him grasp it. Then gently pull away. Repeat this activity a few times.

Hand your baby objects of different sizes, shapes, and textures

Try using terrycloth, silk, blocks, and straws. Brush his fingers with the objects. How long will he hold an object? Will he grab it when it only touches the tips of his fingers?

When your baby's hands respond to even the slightest touch, this is a sign of progress. Now is a good time to introduce easy-to-hold rattles, rings, and other safe objects. By the end of Stage II your baby's grasping will become completely voluntary.

Rattles are wonderful toys, because the sound they make when shaken allows your baby to experience competence. Babies feel a sense of mastery when they are able to control aspects of their environment. This is important not only for their intellectual development, but also for their self-concept. The feedback from the rattle helps your baby adjust his actions and improve his manner of grasping, shaking, and manipulating it.

EYES

Your baby still prefers to look at contours, patterns, and contrasts. Accordingly, it still makes sense to emphasize these features in his bedding, crib accessories, and toys.

The crib bumper we started with (the black and white one with the human faces) will continue to do just fine.

Face time

Since your baby enjoys looking at faces, your face is better than any! Look your baby in the eye, smile, and talk to him; occasionally, make a point of moving from top to bottom and from side to side as you play with him, change him, and follow your daily routine.

Friendly faces

Give your baby stuffed animals or dolls with large faces. Be sure you do not leave these objects in your baby's crib while he sleeps, to avoid possible suffocation.

A new mobile

Change the mobile when your baby's interest seems to wane. Attach brightly colored pieces of paper, cloth, clothes-pins, small bells, and/or large rings to varying lengths of elastic. You might use bright, shiny foil to make a mobile that will reflect light from a window. This will help to develop eye muscle coordination. Use your imagination! Make sure that the mobile is completely safe: it should be high enough so that your baby cannot get tangled in it and made of non-toxic materials.

Follow-the-rattle

Move a rattle from one side of your baby's body to the other, and from top to bottom. Gently shake it as you bring it slowly in a half circle from the center to your baby's left side, back to the center, and then to the right. Be sure that your movements are slow enough to allow your baby to visually follow the rattle, but quick enough to hold his interest.

Light games

In a darkened room, shine a flashlight on the wall, bouncing the light right and left, up and down. Your baby will soon follow the light with his eyes.

Babies enjoy looking at large moving objects. (Any parent who has taken an infant to a restaurant with a ceiling fan can attest to this!) A new mobile or a rod and frame device hung over his crib will both be great fun to watch. To create more visual interest for your baby, hold him so you can both watch people and pets coming and going as you walk around the house. Interacting with others (new faces!) is also fun for your baby: encourage new contacts, such as those with older brothers or sisters. But try to be close by when your baby encounters others. New people may be frightening.

During this stage, your baby will refine his perceptions to the point where he can recognize you, his caretaker, and become aware of himself as separate from other objects and people.

Your baby is becoming aware of himself; he has discovered a new reality. As we have seen, any new discovery needs to be practiced. So help your baby touch his face, feet, eyes, and mouth as you play with him, bathe him, and so on. You can help by holding his hands and bringing them to his cheeks, head, nose, and other parts of his body.

Try tying a small, colorful ribbon or bracelet made of yar around your baby's wrist

This may draw attention to this part of the body. Another variation: place a colorful sock mitten or even a small brightly colored sticker on your baby's hand.

Accommodating

We have seen that as early as the first month your baby can adjust his body to the way you are holding him. No longer the helpless newborn, the Stage II baby can change himself to fit the demands of the situation to some extent— he can accommodate!

Your baby will make many attempts at accommodation now, and our objective in Stage II is to be aware of and support these attempts.

Notice that your baby can now sit and stand briefly while being supported: this is not the "walking reflex" of the newborn, but a new and exciting skill that requires practice. Help your baby stand up and sit while you support him; he will enjoy working on his newfound abilities.

Support your baby in a standing position

Do this for ten to fifteen minutes at a time. Don't overdo it, though.

Hold a shiny foreign object (such as an aluminum pie pan) at arm's length from your baby.

Allow him time to adjust to the new object before bringing it closer. See how your baby reacts to new "ideas." This activity aids in your baby's ability to incorporate novel objects into his "world."

Coordinations

What are the most important examples of coordination at this period? Actually, there are only a few coordinated actions that you need to be aware of. We've already looked at one in some detail: thumb-sucking, part of the coordinated movement of arms and mouth.

At this stage, thumb-sucking is a very common independent activity. Besides occasionally repositioning your baby's hand by his side after a chance contact, there is little you can do to enhance this coordination. Don't worry about discouraging this activity at this age; allow your baby to enjoy his newfound skill.

In playing with your baby, you can help him with his new coordination.

Patty-cake

While your baby is on his back, hold his wrists with your hands and help him with a patty-cake game. Finish the game by moving his hands up to his cheeks so he can explore them. On occasion, bring his hands up to your cheeks instead.

What else is new at Stage II? Your baby's eye coordination rapidly improves. Upon waking, before your baby starts to cry, he may stare at objects dangling overhead, turn his head to follow something moving, and even smile at moving objects or people. You will occasionally see the start of expressed interest in his hands and feet.

In addition to the mobiles and variety shows we have discussed previously, you may now also want to use sound-producing toys or toys that feature bouncing movements. All will help stimulate eye coordination.

An unbreakable mirror

During the later part of Stage II, you can introduce the mirror. Not only is it fun for your baby to gaze at, but it will also help him differentiate himself as an independent object in the world. Your baby will occasionally pound at his image in the mirror. Initially, it may startle him. Then he'll repeat this action again and again. Gradually your baby will develop a distinct sense of himself as separate from other things out there.

You will begin to notice that your baby turns his head in the direction of sound. This action involves a slightly different coordination than that of eye movements and hearing. Your baby will often interrupt his own activity and look attentively in the direction of a sound. Of course, your baby will find some sounds more pleasant than others. Regardless, sounds and sound-producing things are now of great interest to him.

Once you notice your baby turning toward the direction of a sound, you can do a great deal to nurture this new development.

Sound Games

Follow-the-bell

Try repeating the earlier activity of moving an object from side to side using a little bell, or simply snap your fingers as you move a puppet.

Use your voice – Place your baby on his back and face him. Make clicking sounds as you move your face from side to side. Sing, hum, and talk to your baby as you change him and care for him.

Dangle sound-producing toys in front of your baby

Try using toys such as little squeaker balls. Swing the toys gently.

Wind chimes

Hang chimes near a window so your baby hears soft music each time the wind blows through the room.

Play music

Try playing different kinds of music. See what your baby seems to prefer.

Everyday sounds

Expose your baby to a variety of household sounds—vacuum cleaner, doorbells, barking dogs. Provide all sorts of listening stimulation.

When your baby is on his stomach, hold a rattle directly in front of his face

Slowly lift the rattle so that your baby follows the noise by raising his head. Encourage him, if necessary, by gently pushing him up on his hands. Lower the rattle and, as always, repeat.

Vocal Imitation

In Stage II your baby begins to imitate his own utterances and behavior as well as that of others. This important advance means that your baby can remember an event at least long enough to be able to reproduce it.

Little wails may precede crying and are kept up for their own sake. Cooing and gurgling follow. This is the point at which your baby practices vocalizations over and over again, often stopping in surprise then starting the cycle again. Frequently, you may conclude that the only reason he keeps crying is to hear himself vocalize!

In Stage II your baby is beginning to learn for the very first time. He can imitate himself; he can coordinate his actions and produce a repeatable action; and he repeats his actions often enough to develop a habit. These traits herald the beginning of a memory of actions and a sense of physical causality.

Playing a musical instrument is a perfect example of a memory of actions. When I play my guitar, I often try to remember part of a song and mentally reconstruct how it is played, to no avail. But if I start to play the beginning of that song, the rest of it "just comes to me." Another common experience: we all know that once you learn how to ride a bicycle, you always know how. Your baby's "motor memory" is now taking shape. You can nurture this natural tendency in many ways.

Imitate your baby's vocalizations

After you copy your baby, wait for him to produce another sound and then repeat the process. This "communication" exercise encourages your baby to vocalize. Once in a while vary the exercise by changing the sound or the emphasis, tone, or number of repetitions of the utterances. Your baby may even imitate what you do!

You will find that your baby's vocal activity will increase in reaction to the sounds made by others. How can you encourage this ability?

Vary the sound

When you hear your baby making a sound, such as "ah," you can then say a prolonged "aaaah." Soon your baby will, in turn, imitate you.

This form of imitation is limited, of course, to sounds that your baby knows how produce. This once again demonstrates your baby's ability to coordinate events, integrating hearing with vocalizing. Listening to his own voice and vocalizations will often stimulate him to vocalize more. Babies really do enjoy hearing themselves!

Nod your head back and forth and up and down as you speak to your baby

Does your baby try to follow your actions? If he waits until you have stopped before beginning nodding, this shows accommodation. He is studying your moves first and modifying his actions to fit yours.

Sing a musical scale

Does your baby's intonation follow your own?

New Ways of Knowing

As babies develop their intelligence, they gradually construct more elaborate and stable understandings of the reality of their surroundings, a reality founded on their understanding of objects, time, space, and causality. For example, your baby's understanding of an object like a rattle evolves over time and with experience. In his first month of life your baby did not consider the rattle to be a distinct separate object. Now he does.

Compare your knowledge of a rattle with your baby's. Obviously, your understanding of the rattle is much deeper: you know its physical features, its attributes, and how these traits relate to other objects. You know the rattle's price and its function. You also know that just because the rattle falls on the floor out of your sight that does not mean it has vanished from the face of the earth. In contrast, your baby knows that a rattle is something to shake, bang, and put in the mouth. That is all.

As your baby interacts with the rattle, he learns about many aspects of the toy. He realizes that it can be moved (in space), and that this moving happens in time (there is a sequence to his actions—first he grasps the rattle, then shakes it, then bangs it, then puts it in his mouth). He also discovers that shaking the rattle causes a sound—that's the beginning of understanding physical causality, or what causes something to happen. Your child is constructing two kinds of knowledge as he interacts with an object: know-how (the methods of his own abilities) and knowledge of the object itself.

Remember, all thought stems from action. First your baby knows on a working, action plane. Then, and only then, can he internalize or represent that knowledge through an image, word, or sign—to know on a thoughtful level.

Bearing this in mind, let's look again at the your baby's capabilities in Stage II with respect to the categories of knowledge. Unlike Stage I (when your baby had absolutely no notion of the concept of object), Stage II infant development includes coordination of a number of abilities and events, giving your baby a sense of stability. As we have seen, in this stage your baby learns to relate a sound to its source. Repetition of this relation emphasizes the existence of something real, creating a readiness for the object concept, albeit a very premature one.

In Stage II your baby is also just beginning to understand that an object has an existence all its own: your baby looks at the spot where he lost visual contact with the object. For example, let's say you move a rattle in front of your baby and he follows it with his eyes. If you then cover the rattle with your hand, your baby will continue to look at your hand for a short time. He doesn't look for long, and he doesn't visually search for the rattle. But he does watch briefly for the object to reappear.

Active searching for vanished objects is the first real indication that babies understand object permanence. In Stage II your baby does not give us that indication; he shows a kind of passive expectation, expecting the object to be where he last saw it. Your baby has not yet taken the next step, which is to actively search for the object visually. As for his concepts of space, time, and causality, In Stage II he will show similar "small steps," rather than radical changes. Full understanding—even on an exclusively active plane—is yet to come.

The important point to remember is that in Stage II your baby is qualitatively different than he was in Stage I. Whereas his actions in Stage I were purely reflexive, in Stage II he has outgrown this early way of knowing, developing the capability to learn simple actions and to coordinate them, focusing on actions that involve his own body. The increasing control your baby gains over his own body during this stage, coupled with his desire to influence objects in the world around him, will take him directly into Stage III.

SUMMARY OF INTELLECTUAL ATTAINMENTS — STAGE II: ONE TO FOUR MONTHS

AT THE END OF THE FIRST MONTH:

- He prefers contours, patterns, and contrasts.
- His reflexes become more refined.
- He turns his head to look in the direction of a sound.
- He looks attentively at an adult.
- He can adjust his body according to how he is held.

AT THE END OF THE SECOND MONTH:

- He stares at large, moving, contoured objects.
- He responds to people and prefers them to other objects.
- He repeats actions involving his own body (primary circular reaction).
- He looks at his own hand as an object.
- He associates two contiguous events (for example, hearing his mother's voice with eating).
- His eye movements continue to improve.

AT THE END OF THE THIRD MONTH AND THE BEGINNING OF THE FOURTH MONTH:

- His grasping becomes voluntary.
- He establishes hand-eye coordination.
- He becomes aware of himself.
- He orients in the direction of a sound.
- He produces sounds and imitates his own sounds.
- He can sit and stand briefly while supported.

- He recognizes his primary caretaker.
- He swings at nearby objects.

This overview provides an approximate chronological look at important attainments during Stage II; please consider it only as a general guideline. The age range for the appearance of any given attainment is only a rough estimate. Children differ widely in the rate at which they develop, so don't be concerned if your baby does not adhere strictly to these broad standards.

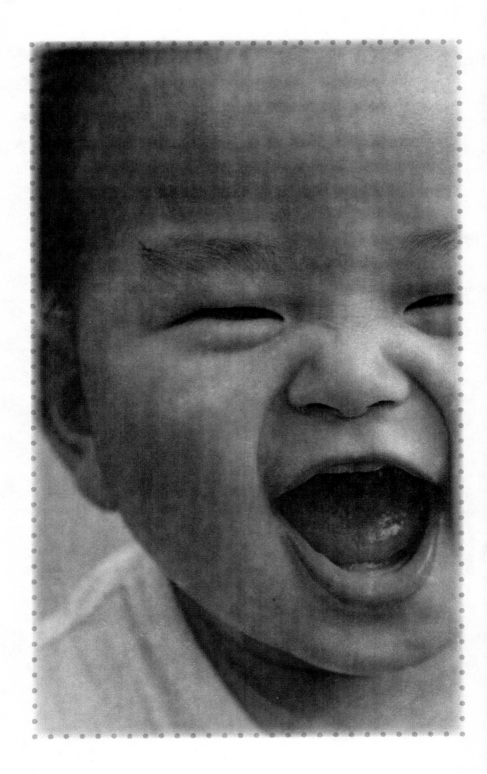

stage 3:

four to eight months

As your baby enters Stage III, her development has progressed beyond body-oriented learning. She now exercises her skills to manipulate the external world of objects. The objective at this stage is to provide her as many opportunities as possible to develop those skills.

During Stage III your baby's physical development will probably progress to include crawling and all that it entails: exploration, discovery, and manipulation of the physical world. Her physical mobility, along with her newly developed ability to coordinate various senses with motor activity, means she is now quite literally ready to reach out to the wondrous world of objects all around her.

Your baby's improved hand-eye coordination permits her to extend her horizon and grasp things she finds within her reach. You might provide easy-to-manipulate objects, such as rattles, rings, wooden spoons, plastic measuring cups, large plastic canisters and their covers, and so on.

SAFETY CHECK

In Stage III, toys take on a greater importance than ever. Toys should be easy for your baby to grasp from any angle, and she should be able to hold them with one hand. Check to make sure there are no sharp edges or loose parts that could detach and pose a choking hazard. Since your baby can reach for things, be sure to dangle or offer only completely safe objects within her reach.

Since almost everything your baby plays with will end up in her mouth, check to make sure toys contain no harmful materials or dyes. It's a good idea to wash toys before playtime as well. Your baby will put her toys through quite an endurance test during this stage, dropping, banging, squeezing, pinching, and chewing them, so it is wise to keep durability in mind when toy shopping. While many of the activities that you did with your baby in Stage I and II will still be appropriate (and fun!), any fragile mobiles and "swallowable" objects used in the early stages must now be removed and replaced with sturdier, larger toys and objects with smooth, safe surfaces.

By the end of Stage III, your baby will be more mobile than ever. As her capabilities increase, be sure to provide a safe space for rolling over, creeping, and crawling. Now is the time to begin baby-proofing (if you haven't already), to make sure your baby's explorations don't put her in harm's way.

Secondary Circular Reactions

Your baby can now reproduce an event that she had caused accidentally and found interesting. For example, your baby may notice that the mobile suspended above her moves when she thrashes her legs around in her crib. She'll thrash around again to try to make the mobile move. If she succeeds, she will repeat the process again and again. Your baby actually enjoys repeating the patterns of behavior she learns!

This pattern of action is called a secondary circular reaction—secondary, because it involves objects beyond your baby's body, and circular, because it is repeated over and over.

When you see evidence of secondary circular reactions, you can be sure that your baby has entered Stage III. A secondary circular reaction may not seem at first glance to be much different than the primary circular reactions of Stage II, but it actually consists of distinct steps. First, your baby accidentally produces an interesting outcome. Next, she perceives a connection between her act and the external outcome. She then repeats the process, and ultimately learns to perform an action that consistently produces the same results.

Here are some ideas on how to help your baby exercise this skill through play.

When your baby perceives a relationship between her act and the resulting event, she is forming a primitive notion of cause and effect, or causality. To reproduce an event, she must construct a practical understanding of means-ends. In other words, she must know that doing this produces that. This brings us to the subject of intention, or whether your baby "means" to do a certain thing.

Use a kick board that has bells attached to it.

Buy a kicking mobile and attach it to your baby's play pen.

Use a jumper seat.

A baby jumper seat helps with the causality concept. Your baby's actions accidentally cause a very interesting result: her own movement!

Hang objects by pieces of elastic above the crib or play pen.

Try to use objects that will produce a noise when your baby hits them. Make sure you supervise your baby during this game, and remove the objects when the play session is over.

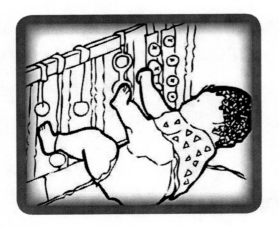

Dangle bells, chimes, rattles, or cloth balls from your baby's crib.

Using these objects increases the chances of her accidentally producing an effect that she can then reproduce on purpose. Be sure each item is attached firmly to the crib rail, and use only short lengths of ribbon or string to ensure your baby doesn't become entangled.

Attach a toy to a short string and place the string in your baby's hand.

Use a variety of toys, such as a tambourine, a bell, noise-makers, and squeakers, as well as silent objects.

Encourage your baby to splash around in the bathtub.

This will help her realize that her motions cause ripples in the water.

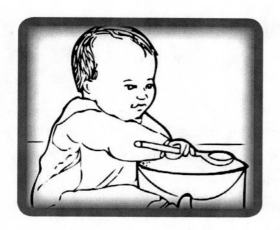

Give your baby a wooden spoon and a pot.

She will discover that hitting the pot with the spoon produces an exciting new noise. Give your baby different pots, pans, and other objects that produce varying noises when hit.

Semi-Intentional Actions

Can we speak, at this stage, of intention on the part of a baby?

To return to our earlier example, your baby thrashes around and notices that the mobile above her crib turns. Later, she repeats the actions to produce the same result. Are her actions intentional?

Is your baby's "meaning" to turn her mobile similar in any way to your intention to, say, drive into town once you get in your car in the morning? The answer is yes: a form of intentionality must certainly be present. She tried to repeat actions that produced interesting outcomes. The intention in question is not fully developed, however, because your baby first only caused the mobile to turn accidentally. Had she thought of the goal first, and then initiated the action to realize it, the act would have been fully intentional.

Secondary circular reactions, such as repeating the motion necessary to make water splash agreeable—and, at first, surprisingly—in the bathtub, are limited in nature. They reproduce events that were brought about by chance. As such, these actions cannot be fully intentional, because your baby did not invent them.

Such actions, far from being inventive, are repetitions of efforts your baby is already capable of doing. We can describe these actions as semi-intentional. This is a good time to play with toys that you and your baby can have some predictable influence on.

Pull a toy to draw it nearer to you and baby.

Roll a ball back and forth.

Shake the crib rail to make your baby's mobile turn.

You can also turn these semi-intentional action games into occasions for social play:

Pull a string to ring a bell.

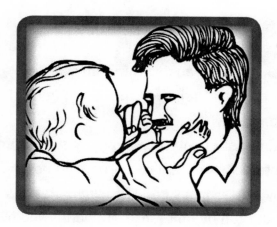

Puff up your cheeks and, taking your baby's hands, bring them against your cheeks to let the air out.

Bring your baby's hands to your mouth while you make a babbling sound.

Children are absolutely delighted with this kind of play. No matter which game you play, make sure that you repeat the same pattern over and over again. Your baby will tell you when you are overdoing it—she will turn the game off by refusing to focus on it!

This is also a good time for vocal imitation games, as your baby continues to imitate sounds she had produced before. Be alert for your baby's utterances and her own imitations of them. Then join in the fun by imitating her sounds and by varying them slightly to see if she follows your lead.

Hands are the key elements in Stage III development. Your baby can now grasp and release an object at will. She shows great interest in grasping and, increasingly, manipulating objects and events in the outside world. She now has greater control over hand movements and much better hand-eye coordination.

In Stage II, your baby explored things mainly with her eyes. In Stage III, her hands do the exploring, and they are every-where, touching, holding, and manipulating.

Help your baby move.

Help your baby crawl. Place her in jumper seats to discover how her actions can result in an outcome.

Show your baby a push and pop toy or a colorful pinwheel to introduce her to new sounds and movements.

Your baby likes to relate her new learning to what she already knows. As you play with your Stage III baby, be prepared to see some "old favorites" take a few surprising turns.

Everything old is new again.

Rolling a ball or pulling a familiar toy in front of your baby may result in a fascinated reappraisal of the object. Allow her to pick up small objects with her fingers; this stimulates small hand muscles and hand-eye coordination.

Nesting objects.

Your baby now gets a great deal of pleasure from taking things apart. Playing with a set of small pots and pans is a great source of learning and fun. Put one pot inside another, then separate them. Don't be surprised if she can't put them back together. That will come later!

Color your world.

Babies begin to distinguish colors between the ages of six and twelve months. Use your felt banner (from Chapter 7) to introduce brightly colored pictures and shapes. Talk to your baby as you point out the different colors. Emphasize colors in all of your daily activities: choose colorful towels forbathing, solid colored toys and objects, colored plastic flatware, etc.

Earlier, your baby displayed an interest in her hands. Now help her to discover her feet as well.

Where are baby's toes?

With your baby lying on her back, brush her toes with a
rattle few times. Does she extend her leg and kick? Raise the
rattle higher, and then sweep it right and left. Can your baby
coordinate her actions to move her feet closer to the rattle?
You should note that her understanding of her hands does
not always extend to her feet.

Toy makeover.

Present a toy that is actually old but appears new. You might, for instance, attach a bell to a rubber duck. Normally your baby produces a "bell noise" by shaking the bell and a "duck noise" by squeezing the duck. What is her reaction to producing a noise by shaking the duck?

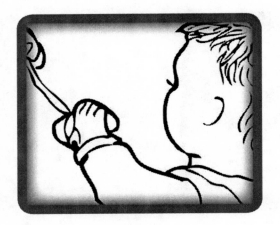

Baby tug-of-war.

Pull and stretch games are very good at this age. Connect two cloth balls with a short piece of elastic. Hold one end and encourage your baby to hold the other. Stretch the elastic and release.

Explore textures

Give your baby a series of objects to handle—first hard things, then soft, then fuzzy. Talk to her about each one. Your words are not so much for the sake of teaching her language as they are for teaching her that words are used to name things.

The Object Concept Gets Stronger

Early in Stage III, if you drop a rattle in front of your baby, chances are she won't watch as it falls. But later in this stage (at approximately seven months), if she sees the start of the rattle's fall, your baby will look around on the blanket in front of her to find it.

This visual searching for a vanished object marks your baby's evolving understanding of object permanence. For instance, your baby might drop a set of plastic keys, and then look around for them. Furthermore, if she spots part of the keys, she understands that the rest of the toy is hidden, and yes, she will definitely want to find it! Conversely, if she doesn't see any part of the keys, she will abandon the visual search.

Your baby goes through several steps in understanding that objects have permanence. In Stage II, we saw that she demonstrated no visual search for vanished objects. In Stage III your baby does search visually, and in Stage IV your baby will search manually for a disappearing object.

Your baby's memory has evolved, too. She can now distinguish between old things and new ones. Though you are introducing new toys, you may want to keep some old ones. However, once your baby no longer shows any interest in a toy, you may wish to give it away.

People Learning

During Stage III, social interaction profoundly stimulates your baby's intellect.

Mirror Image

Fasten a non-breakable mirror to the crib bumper so your baby can respond to her own image and further understand her own separate identity. Try standing with your baby in your arms in front of a mirror so that she can see both of your faces.

At this stage, the greatest wonder and delight are brought out by the game of peek-a-boo. Playing a variety of peek-a-boo games provides an excellent opportunity for your baby to exercise her understanding of object permanence. For the four-to-eight-month-old, the experience seems magical. How can something disappear (for them, cease to exist!) only to appear again?

Peek-a-boo games in which your baby can see a part of you (while the rest is hidden) confirm her newly established expectation that the rest of you can be found. You will find that your baby's instinct is to play the game over and over again; do not deny her. Enjoy the thrill that your baby experiences.

A variety of peek-a-boo games will help stimulate development and are lots of fun for your baby.

Where will it land?

Since your baby will visually follow a falling object until it stops, show her a small, light plastic rattle and drop it in front of her. Repeat this and watch your baby's eyes to see if she anticipates the rattle's fall to its resting position.

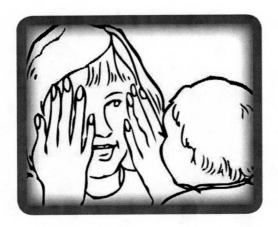

Hidden face.

In the initial phases of Stage III, play peek-a-boo games in which you hide your face, revealing a small portion of it.

Hidden toy.

Later, play the game by hiding a toy behind an object, partially revealing a portion of it.

Visual search.

Later in Stage III, your baby will visually search for a vanished object. Hide an object, such as a set of plastic keys,
behind a pillow. Draw your baby's attention to the keys,
and when she focuses on them, cover them with a blanket.
Uncover them while your baby is still watching.

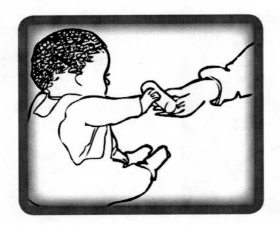

Where did it go?

By the end of this period your baby searches for an object that she had been holding by continuing the same gripping movement. Slip a toy out of your baby's hand. Watch for the grasping movements, and then place the toy back in your baby's hand.

Spatial Relations

Stage III affords you an opportunity to expand on your baby's spatial concepts, as well. Here are some suggestions:

Reach for it!

Instead of simply placing objects in your baby's hands, try bringing them slowly within reach. How close must an object be before she'll reach for it? Does the distance vary depending on the size of the object?

Moving rattle.

Move a rattle so that your baby must reach first in front of her, then to the right, then to the left, then up in the air. This helps encourage reaching.

Batting practice.

Give your baby a spoon, a toothbrush, and a comb, and then dangle a baby shoe in front of her by its lace. Allow your baby to discover how the varying intensity of her swings affects the shoe when it is hit.

Where is the toy?

While looking in the mirror, show your baby the reflection of a toy. Then move the toy behind her, still keeping it visible in the mirror. Where does your baby reach when she can only see the toy in the mirror?

Moving On

The distinct attainments of each stage offer you an idea of the remarkable growth patterns in your child's mind. However, keep in mind that all of these developments are gradual, like images coming steadily into focus rather than lights being suddenly switched on. By the end of Stage III, your baby will see herself as a means to various ends. She will know that she can cause things to happen, and will derive tremendous pleasure from practicing her new, steadily growing mental powers. In Stage IV she will perfect her understanding of cause and effect relationships, and she will use her increasingly sophisticated knowledge of the world around her to select her own ways to achieve predetermined goals. Let your natural instincts and your knowledge of your own baby be your primary guide as you interact with her. Most of all, enjoy the fun that comes with thinking up activities for your baby's intellectual enhancement.

SUMMARY OF INTELLECTUAL ATTAINMENTS — STAGE III: FOUR TO EIGHT MONTHS

AT THE END OF THE FOURTH MONTH:

- She reproduces an environmental outcome originally produced by chance (secondary circular reaction).
- She begins to manipulate objects.
- She recognizes the relationship between acts and outcomes.
- She repeats newly learned behavior patterns.
- She distinguishes new toys from old toys.
- She continues to imitate sounds she had produced before.

AT THE END OF THE FIFTH MONTH:

- She reaches for an object.
- She anticipates an entire object by seeing only part of it.

AT THE END OF THE SIXTH MONTH:

- She is interested in containers.
- She visually anticipates the resting position of falling objects.
- She visually searches for a vanished object.

AT THE END OF THE SEVENTH MONTH AND THE BEGINNING OF THE EIGHTH MONTH:

- She reaches for, grasps, manipulates, and mouths objects.
- She responds to her mirror image.
- She searches for an object that she grasped and dropped by continuing the same grasping movements.

It is worth repeating that the age at which children attain and master any process varies. Please consider age approximations as rough estimates only.

stage 4:

eight to twelve months

As we have seen, infant growth is a subtle, incremental thing. However gradual the changes may be, though, virtually all parents experience sudden awe and wonder when they consider their baby's accomplishments by the fourth stage of intellectual growth. Just a few months ago, your baby was an essentially passive, reflex-dependent being. How much has changed!

In Stage III your baby showed enormous and rapid learning, but in Stage IV your baby consolidates and reconciles past attainments and extends them to apply to new and different situations. Thus the special mental attainments of Stage IV have their roots in Stage III and are outgrowths of skills developed earlier. This is an exciting time for both you and your baby.

In Stage III, your baby learned to reproduce interesting effects on the objects around him (the secondary circular reactions we learned about earlier). Stage IV is characterized by deferred circular reactions, where your baby can stop his own repetitive actions to pay attention to another event, and then start over again.

For example, suppose your baby is crawling toward a toy. You interrupt him by calling to him. He stops, looks at you, but then continues crawling toward the toy. The beauty of the deferred circular reaction is that it clearly shows the substantial improvement in memory now at your baby's disposal.

SAFETY CHECK

Between the ages of eight and twelve months, most babies learn to crawl and to pull themselves up to a standing position. Many begin walking while holding on to furniture, known as "cruising," and some may even begin to walk independently.

Your baby's higher reach may enable him to grab previously inaccessible objects, so be sure that dangerous objects and breakables are up out of his reach and that cabinets and drawers at his level are securely locked. You may also want to pad any sharp corners or edges in his play area (low table edges or hearths, for example) to protect against possible injury as your baby takes his early steps.

The Dawn of Full Intent and Other Milestones

Your baby will now work on perfecting a number of major attainments, beginning with the concept of means-ends relations. Now your baby thinks of a means to accomplish goals. Your baby shows clear signs of elementary planning. You may see him, for instance move one object out of his way to get another.

Along other lines, previously your baby learned to visually search for a vanished object. Now when an object vanishes from his field of vision, your baby will search for it manually as well as visually, clearly demonstrating his understanding that objects can exist independently of his own direct perception of them. This shows an important improvement of his understanding that objects that go out of sight do not necessarily vanish altogether.

Your baby's talent for imitation has progressed to the point where he can reproduce an action involving parts of his body he cannot see. This ability is crucial because it allows your baby to accommodate himself to new situations. Such adjustments are a further sign of adaptability, which as we know, is the essence of all intelligence.

Your baby also shows greater anticipation of events. He has learned to associate certain events to other events immediately preceding them, and will react with surprise when his expectations aren't met.

Finally, the Stage IV baby has grown to understand that not only can he be the source of activity, but other objects and other people can also cause things to happen. This insight is fundamental for a full understanding of cause-effect relations.

As your baby puts these forms of intelligent actions to work, he builds his knowledge of reality. He knows that the hidden object he wishes to see again exists somewhere, and he searches for it with his hands near where it was last seen. Your baby has also developed his concepts of space and time more fully, understanding on a practical level such concepts as "in," "out," "behind," and "through." All this knowledge works together to bring him a richer and fuller understanding of the world than he has ever known.

Let's take a closer look at each of the prominent Stage IV abilites.

Means-Ends Relations

Adults tend to take the idea of means and ends for granted. For instance, we assume that turning on the television set will result in a picture. For your baby, such patterns of implicit relationships are only beginning to emerge. Previously his world was characterized for the most part by a series of seemingly random and unconnected events. Now your baby confirms his recent suspicion that there is more to this series of surprises than meets the eye, and he uses that knowledge to his advantage.

Our first concrete sign that a baby has entered Stage IV occurs when he demonstrates the ability to intentionally select a means in order to attain a pre-established goal.

In a classic example of this development, Piaget described how he showed an object to his son Laurent, but placed his hand in front of it, leaving the object only partially visible. At seven months, seventeen days of age, Laurent tried to get the object by hitting his father's hand. At nine months, fifteen days, he pushed Piaget's hand away with one hand and grabbed the object with the other.

Laurent conceived the means (pushing Daddy's hand away) before reaching the goal (getting the object). This ability is what distinguishes the Stage IV baby from his previous ways of interacting with the world, and you can be sure that from this point forward your baby will eagerly look for new ways to reach his goals. In fact, you should probably enjoy this resourcefulness while it operates on a comparatively small scale. In a year or so, you will be both amazed and exhausted at the apparently limitless resolve your child will show in attempting to attain his goals!

INTENTIONAL OR NOT?

How do you know your baby's actions are intentional? Try a simple experiment:

With your baby focused on what you are doing, throw a set of plastic keys in front of him. His first reaction will be to reach for the keys and chew on them. Now throw the keys behind a pillow. What will he do?

He will probably react one of two ways: he will cry in anger and frustration, or he will push the pillow away so he can grab the keys.

If your baby cries, he simply has a little more developing to do. If he retrieves the keys, he is showing with great authority that he has already developed the capacity for intentional action. His solution of this problem illustrates the remarkable ability of a Stage IV baby to construct a plan to pass over an obstacle.

Don't be alarmed if your eight-month-old doesn't solve this problem. Remember, we are not in a race. Children are all different, and their intellectual development will vary somewhat. Minor variations from the norm are nothing to fret over.

Solving the missing-object problem illustrates the remarkable ability of your Stage IV baby to construct a mental bridge, of sorts, in order to pass over a recognized obstacle. You can be sure your baby's actions are intentional when:

• He uses an indirect approach to reach a goal when some obstacle prevents him from achieving it.

- He doesn't stumble accidentally upon the goal while playing but shows signs he conceived of the goal before he initiated the action to reach it.

- He overcomes the obstacle by different means than the ones he normally uses to reach his goal.

Our experiment with the plastic keys passes all three tests. Your baby attempted to get the keys directly by grabbing them, but was stopped by the pillow. He had to think of pushing away the pillow to reach the keys. Thus he figured out a new solution to his problem.

You can also try replicating Piaget's experiment with his son Laurent. Attract your baby's interest with a rattle, and then place your hand in front of it, preventing him from reaching and grasping it directly. If his response to the problem is to push aside your hand, then his action is fully intentional.

You will also start to notice day-to-day examples in your baby's activity. I often sit on the sofa at home with my legs up on the coffee table. At five months, if my daughter Beth wanted to get a toy on the other side of me, she would show anger and frustration, not knowing how to get around the obstacle. By eight months or so she would simply crawl under my legs and get the toy. In that instance, Beth showed evidence of a pre-established means to attaining a goal, that is, of fully intentional action.

Try to engage your baby in plenty of activities to enrich his thinking about "if-this-then-that" concepts and nurture her understanding of means-ends relationships.

Here are a few simple ideas:

Attach a strand of ribbon to a rattle and place the strand in your baby's hand.

Help your baby pull on the ribbon, causing the rattle to shake and draw closer and closer to him. In the beginning, be sure he sees and hears the rattle being dragged forward. Later, repeat this game, but hide the rattle under a cover and then pull it. This will strengthen two different schemes: means-ends and object permanence. You can also play these games with a small pull toy.

- Help your baby play with a jack-in-the-box.
- Roll toy cars and trucks over a smooth surface.
- Roll around large striped balls.
- Stack blocks to build a tower and then knock it down.
- Help your baby wind a wind-up toy and then release it.

These kinds of activities foster several developing abilities. For example, your baby discovers cause and effect in realizing he can cause a bell to ring.

Other games along these lines include the following:

Music boxes.

Music boxes are wonderful at this stage. Does your baby realize that the box must be wound in order for the music to play?

Block train.

Place three blocks in a row and encourage your baby to push them around. His actions will help him realize that pushing the end block makes all the others move as well.

Pat-a-cake.

At nine months, your baby enjoys playing pat-a-cake and similar games. Speak clearly as you play. Use rhymes and rhythm games.

Rhythm instruments.

Expose your baby to instruments such as drums, maracas, and xylophones. Will he make the connection between the hitting or shaking and the resulting noise?

Hand it over!

Hand your baby a toy but continue to hold one end of it. Does he try to hit your hand to make you release the toy? This helps your baby realize that your hands as well as his can be used as a means to an end.

Imitation

In Stage IV your baby shows considerable progress in the area of imitation. Consider this example: At about eight months of age, my daughter Beth would vocalize various sounds. One day I heard her saying "a-wa-wa" over and over. I repeated it immediately, several times. She looked up at me, and once I stopped, she started to imitate me. I quickly changed the utterance to "a-wa-wa-wa." Again she stopped, noticing the change. When I stopped, she took her turn, repeating the new variation. In order to achieve this imitation, Beth had to use parts of her body she couldn't see (her tongue and mouth) and equally important, she showed that she could imitate the new sounds I had made.

Your baby may not always be able to imitate you exactly. If you bend your finger in a certain way, the closest your baby may be able to come will be to wave his arm! Still, this shows that your baby is now aware of the movements of his own body as well as the movements of others. Although Beth could not see her tongue and mouth movements in relation to mine, she could feel them. She made a connection between what she had seen me do and what she could not see herself do.

Keep in mind that at this stage your baby is only capable of imitating movements that are familiar actions already in his repertoire. Furthermore, his initial attempts at imitation are usually only approximate reproductions.

Now your baby has improved memory for concrete events and can imitate actions and sounds that took place earlier. He can also postpone an action that he had initiated, pay attention to another event, and then resume his action pattern again. He will enjoy playing the following imitation games.

Funny faces.

Make faces and wait for your baby's imitation. Also: Repeat sounds that your baby utters. Change a feature of the utterance, such as the number of times you repeat the sound or the length of the utterance.

Point to and name objects in picture books while telling the story.

Encourage your baby to feed you, wipe your face with a towel, etc.

Head scratching.

Scratch your head dramatically, exaggerating the motions.
Wait for your baby to imitate you.

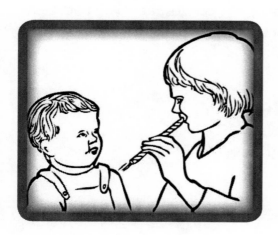

Straw games.

Blow air through a straw. Can your baby imitate this action?

Take a call.

Give your baby a block or paper tube. Dial the phone. Does he try to imitate your actions? Later on, does your baby use a toy telephone to try to imitate you? Does he try to imitate your playing the piano? Try hugging a stuffed animal. Does he stop what he is doing in order to watch you and then return to his previous activity?

Later in Stage IV your baby can start to imitate your original actions. Be inventive and give him plenty of actions to choose from. Some suggestions:

- Yawn.
- Wave bye-bye.
- Clap your hands.
- Make animal noises.
- Stick out your tongue.
- Rub your eyes.
- Touch your toes.

Anticipation

In Stage IV your baby will show an increasing ability to anticipate events. Anticipations result from established routines. Certain visual cues or other stimuli alert your baby to a familiar pattern and signal a forthcoming event. For example, your baby may start to cry when he sees the babysitter, knowing that it means you will soon be leaving.

One of my students at UCLA followed a few routines with her baby. When she made her bed in the morning, she would put the pillows at the foot of the bed and fluff them up. Her son, Andrew, would squeal with delight each day as he slapped the pillows. When Andy saw his mother preparing to make the bed, he eagerly awaited the pillows at the foot of the bed so he could slap and fluff! Also, whenever she changed Andy's diaper or dressed him on the changing table, my student turned on the tape recorder located behind the changing table. If she did not turn the tape on immediately, Andy would turn his head to look directly at the tape recorder. He knew that a diaper change meant music!

Setting up routines and playing the same games over and over again helps nurture your baby's ability to anticipate. For example, playing "this little piggy" or similar tickle games helps your baby learn what to expect.

My daughter Beth enjoyed playing the airplane game: I would make the whining sound of an airplane engine and then swoop in to "attack," ending up with my head in her lap. We both enjoyed the game. Yet at the same time Beth was firmly constructing the concept of anticipation: the moment I made the airplane noise, she would perk up and prepare for the game.

Where did it go?

Hold your baby on your lap and drop a toy on the floor, then ask him, "Where did the toy go?"

What comes next?

Can your baby anticipate events? Walk toward him with a bib and put it on him. Does he squeal or elevate his shoulders in anticipation of mealtime? Approach him with a favorite toy. Does he get excited as he concentrates on the object?

Learn wherever you go.

Make daily routines into exciting learning experiences. For example, in the supermarket, have your baby help you place things in the cart. Point out color, size, texture (fruits and vegetables are good for this), and the pictures on the boxes. This will help him to connect the picture on the outside with the object on the inside.

Physical Causality
. . . .

Before Stage IV, you may have thought to yourself that
your baby seemed self-centered or even egocentric, to use
an admittedly adult way of looking at things. To our way of
thinking, at least, this was a very accurate analysis. After all,
if we meet an adult who seems to believe that his actions and
only his actions cause things to occur, we consider that person
rather self-absorbed. That self-absorption is the frame of
reference your baby has been operating under for the first
three stages.

In Stage IV, for the first time, your baby becomes aware
that objects can cause actions to occur, or that another
person can initiate an event. Your Stage IV baby is far from
being a picture of altruism. However, his egocentricity does
seem to have receded noticeably. This is because the world
as experienced by your baby has taken on an entirely new
feel since his discovery that he is not the only one who
initiates action.

I once played a game with Beth in which I lightly pinched
her nose and said "honk, honk." When I removed my hand,
she would quickly grab it and place it on her nose so that
I would repeat the game. She had obviously established a
cause-effect connection: she realized that the cause was
pinching the nose, and the effect was saying "honk, honk."

Similarly, if your baby realizes that you have to wind a
wind-up toy in order to make it perform, then he has realized a cause-effect relation that goes beyond his causing an

event. Your winding the toy (cause) makes the toy perform (effect). For the very first time, causality has been externalized.

Here are a few game suggestions to help develop your baby's sense of physical causality.

Roll a ball roughly the size of a volleyball to knock down a doll as your baby watches.

Strike a small drum.

Using a drum will help your baby connect the sounds with the arm movements that produce them.

Let your baby turn the dial on an old radio to change the station.

Make marks on a small chalkboard.

Assist your baby in playing with toy trucks and cars.

Object Concept

Somewhere between the ages of eight to ten months your baby will reach another milestone: he will finally master the concept of object permanence. When an object vanishes from his field of vision, he will search for it both visually and manually. If you drop a toy in front of your baby now and immediately cover it with a handkerchief, he will pull away the hanky to get the toy.

In Stage III, your baby's object concept was developing. He might have looked around for a missing object, but his understanding had not yet matured to the point where manual search was possible. Now your baby clearly demonstrates his understanding that objects can exist independently of his own direct perception of them.

Interestingly, this ability has certain limitations. Suppose, when you and your baby are playing with blocks, he sees you put some blocks in the side compartment of his rolling toy cart. At this stage he will lift the cart top and retrieve the blocks. But if you were first to put the blocks in the cart, then remove them, and then put them under a blanket, with your baby watching you the entire time, he would be unable to retrieve the blocks from the second hiding place.

We describe this limitation by saying that in Stage IV, sequential displacement has not yet developed. Remember, ideas are not mastered instantaneously. It will take some time for your baby to refine his perceptions of the world. Your baby needs practice in manually searching for objects in order for the object concept to develop to the next level of sophistication.

Again, peek-a-boo type games are an excellent way to enrich the concept of object permanence. A word of caution: be careful not to startle your baby by placing his blanket over his head.

Hide an object in a cooking pot with a cover and let your baby retrieve it.

Put a ticking clock under your baby's blanket and let him search for and un

Opening "presents."

Wrap a noise-making toy such as a rattle in a piece of paper or a piece of cloth, then help your baby unwrap it.

Nesting toys.

Let your baby play with cups that fit into one another, or a series of concentric cylinders that collapse into one another and pull out to form a cone.

Hide objects as your baby watches. Let her find them.

In and out.

Supervise while your baby places small objects in a jar and removes them. Vary the game by using a pot, a bag, or a shoebox.

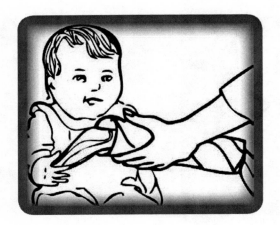

Hide a handkerchief.

Use a cardboard tube from a roll of paper towels and slip a colorful handkerchief through one end and out the other as your baby watches. Help him do it too.

Use different barriers in covering objects.

Try boxes, books, paper, blankets, clothes, pans, pillows, cups, stuffed animals, your entire body, your legs, etc. Also try placing the barrier so that if your baby knocks too hard, the concealed toy will fall out of reach. This will help him learn to control his arm movements.

Hidden doll.

In peek-a-boo games, place a doll under a blanket so that
its shape is visible but no part of the doll actually shows.
Later try placing the doll under a box so it is completely
hidden. Will your baby search for the doll?

Different hiding places.

Put a toy in a paper bag, then a cloth bag, then a shoebox, then a round box. Let your baby watch you find the toy. Repeat the procedure and see if he makes any gestures to find the object himself. Try dropping the toy into a sock.

Rattle hide-and-seek.

Play hide-and-seek by placing a rattle under a box and shaking the rattle gently. Does this help your baby to search for the object?

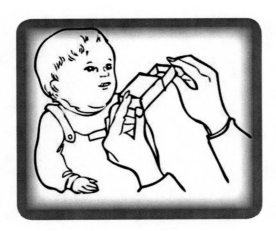

Matchbox hide-and-seek.

Play hide-and-seek with a matchbox that slides in and out. This is a more complicated variation on the theme.

Clothes will provide many interesting opportunities for peek-a-boo activities as you dress and undress your baby. By the way, it may be frustrating from your point of view, but the baby who takes off his diapers and pants is demonstrating a new ability to remove barriers.

Your baby's intelligent actions cannot be performed in a vacuum; they must be performed on what I have referred to as "objects of knowledge." Space and time are also objects of knowledge. Here are some games you can try at this stage to enhance your baby's understanding of how objects behave in space and in time. (If you are thinking to yourself that this sounds like the beginnings of physics, you're right!)

Fill up and empty boxes.

Let your baby play with sponges in the bathtub.

Cut a hole in the top of a large coffee can and help your baby drop cereal inside.

Coordinating and Consolidating

In Stage IV your baby is less interested in learning new schemes than in discovering how to apply what he already knows to new situations. This is an opportunity for you to help your baby consolidate his past experiences.

Throughout his development, your baby has been making sense of the physical, logical, and cultural world he lives in by acting on things and by seeing other people acting on things. He constructs his own knowledge of scientific and mathematical principles by acting on the objects around him, and creates knowledge of the social world surrounding him by observing language, cultural expectations, daily routines, and other rules. As your child moves out of babyhood, he will use his knowledge to begin experimenting on his surroundings, using trial and error to discover new sequences of actions to solve problems. In short, in Stage V you will witness your toddler's creativity blossom.

SUMMARY OF INTELLECTUAL ATTAINMENTS —
STAGE IV: EIGHT THROUGH TWELVE MONTHS AT THE END
OF THE EIGHTH MONTH:

- She visually searches for a vanished object.
- His actions become fully intentional.
- He explores objects, appreciating that their existence is separate from his own.
- He manually searches for hidden objects when he can see them being hidden.
- He solves simple problems by isolating means from their ends; in other words, he selects his goal first, and then figures out a way to achieve it.
- He has improved memory for concrete events, and can imitate actions and sounds that took place earlier.
- He can stop one activity to pay attention to something else, and then return to the first activity (deferred circular reactions).
- He begins to see himself as the means to various ends.

AT THE END OF THE NINTH MONTH:

- His object concept continues to mature; he knows a hidden object will reappear.
- He establishes herself as a causal agent.

AT THE END OF THE TENTH MONTH:

- He manually searches for a vanished object that was hidden in his view.
- He imitates regularly observed acts.

- He perceives himself as separate from other objects.
- He anticipates regular routines.

AT THE END OF THE ELEVENTH MONTH AND BEGINNING OF THE TWELFTH MONTH:

- He experiments with the spatial relations of objects. For example, he will nest things into one another.
- He imitates more subtle movements.
- He shows his capacity to image some events by his improved ability to remember.

Please remember that these age approximations are rough estimates only. Normal development allows for a wide range of behavior, and your baby will progress in his own unique way.

stage 5:
twelve to eighteen months

Happy Birthday! Congratulations to you and your child. Throughout this year your baby has steadily progressed from a state of near-total helplessness to one of dawning mental awareness of the physical and social world around her. In short, your baby is now a toddler.

Your child is beginning to walk, talk, and even solve problems on a sensorimotor level. Now that she has reached these milestones, we have only two infant stages left to discuss, Stages V and VI—probably the most extraordinary periods of all. By the conclusion of Stage V, your child will display her first authentic, purposeful, individually creative experimentation. Her entry to Stage VI will mark the beginning of what we can legitimately call independent thought.

SAFETY CHECK

If your child wasn't walking before, she will almost certainly begin walking during Stage V. Provide a safe environment for her to practice her new skill by removing objects that might trip her up, such as loose throw rugs, and pad sharp furniture edges to protect against injury in her inevitable falls.

Your child may also become interested in climbing. Make sure furniture such as dressers and bookcases are anchored to the wall or are otherwise tip-proof; your child's weight can cause objects such as these to topple onto her if she tries to scale them. Her climbing skills may also give her access to items previously out of reach. At this age you may no longer be able to anticipate every possible danger your child may get into, so there is no substitute for close supervision.

Tertiary Circular Reactions

Watch your child drop a spoon and pick it up again. You may notice that she repeats this action over and over again, each time concentrating on the way she releases the spoon and where it lands.

Your child is trying to understand the "know-how of experimentation." She systematically varies previously learned and well-patterned behavior to discover what the new results might be. Already familiar with the outcome of a given sequence of behavior, your child makes small procedural changes in an effort to see what effect the changes produce.

Piaget labeled this the stage of tertiary circular reactions. In secondary circular reactions, your child repeated the exact same action to confirm knowledge she gained in previous experiments. In tertiary circular reactions, your child causes something to happen accidentally but repeats the action by deliberately and systematically varying it to monitor expected changes in outcome. Tertiary circular reactions are intentional, repetitive, experimental action patterns.

If you look closely at your child's actions, you will agree that her interest in novelty drives her to experiment. She has become a dauntless researcher, resorting to endless trial and error to test final results. The vital issue on your child's mind now is how she has affected the outside world.

While secondary circular reactions were meant to consolidate the processes of experimentation, tertiary circular reactions extend them in an effort to find limits. In how many different situations does a certain sequence of actions accomplish something? How can you adapt that sequence of actions to fit other situations?

These are profound questions for your child, and she toils ceaselessly now to find answers to them. Here's what you can do to enrich this experimental bent in your baby.

Playing with gravity.

At this age, your child likes to throw things. Set an object on the corner of her playpen so that she can knock it off. Retrieve the object and repeat the game, placing the object elsewhere on the next turn. Use different objects of varying weights. Show your child a small "bobo doll," an inflatable toy weighted to keep it standing upright. Push the doll gently in one direction and then in another. Let your child try to do the same.

Swing a ball.

Place a ball in the end of an old nylon stocking and swing it around in front of your child. Does she try to swing it too? Hold the stocking in front of your child and encourage her to push it around to see how it swings back and forth.

Ramps.

Set up a variety of inclines and provide your child with some toys that roll, such as balls and cars. Vary the angle to see different results. Lay the board flat on the floor and roll a car over it. Then move one end of the board up slightly to increase the angle of the incline and roll the car over it. Repeat. Then let your child roll the car.

Let your child build things.

Provide a variety of building materials for your child, such as books, cardboard paper tubes, blocks, or foam shapes. Encourage her to experiment with these items by stacking them, rolling them, and fitting them into each other.

Examine properties of the world around you.

Encourage your child to discover physical resistance by taking her outside and rolling a ball in the grass, where it doesn't roll as well. Also, try dropping different types of balls on a variety of surfaces, such as shag rugs, plastic placemats, smooth sheets, or sand.

Compare real objects to pictures.

Cut out pictures of everyday objects such as apples, balls, and cups. Then place examples of the actual objects by the pictures. Can you help your child to match real objects with their pictures?

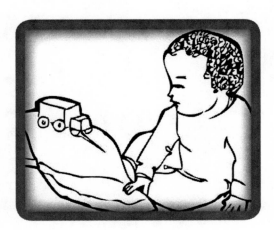

Place a toy on a towel so that your child must tug on the towel to get the object.

Water play

In a sandbox or at the kitchen sink, experiment with pouring water and sand or mud.

Give your child a plastic screw-top jar to fill and empty, open and close.

More is better.

Children at this stage enjoy playing with quantities of the same item. Try to accommodate this by giving your child several pillows or balls, lots of large buttons, spools, jar lids, etc.

Give your child large wooden beads to slide on a straw.

Problem Solving by Discovery

In Stage V, your child displays intelligence by discovering entirely new sequences of actions in order to solve problems. Try the following experiment: place a toy on a blanket about three feet away from your child, and restrain her so she can't get the toy. What will she do? When she fails to get the toy simply by reaching for it, she may then pull the blanket to bring the toy within reach. If you then place another toy on the blanket, she'll go through the same motions again, first reaching for the toy, then resorting to the more elaborate scheme of pulling the blanket.

Inventing new sequences of action in an effort to deal with new situations is what this stage is all about. This is the beginning of creative and internally intelligent behavior.

Obviously, children are not always able to solve problems with foresight. What happens when they encounter more difficult problems? Now they can resort to trial-and-error, a strategy that had not been available to them up to now.

At this stage, when your child is faced with a problem that cannot be solved by inventing a new sequence of behavior through foresight and pre-planning, she experiments in a hit-or-miss style until she stumbles on a solution. This activity is not mindless; it involves a strategy of trying alternative solutions that maximizes the chance of success through physical groping. In this sense your one-year-old begins to show the characteristics of a true problem solver!

Piaget described his own daughter, Jacqueline, demonstrating this technique when she was fifteen months old.
She had thrown a stuffed dog outside the bars of her playpen, and when she attempted to reach for it, she inadvertently
pushed her playpen toward the toy. Then she accidentally
moved it in the wrong direction. She immediately set the
playpen back on the correct course and got the dog. Jacqueline used her fortuitous discoveries to invent a new way
of reaching her goal, shaping her trial and error into a new,
systematic effort.

You can encourage your baby at this stage by helping her
discover the workings of hammer boards, merry-go-rounds,
"corn popper" push toys, pop-up men, and pinwheels.

Intention and Means-Ends Relations

The Stage V child carries out an action and interprets the
results according to what she already knows. Never pas-

sive, she continually monitors the results of her actions and adapts subsequent actions accordingly.

In the toy-on-the-blanket example, your child demonstrated an intentional plan to use a specific means in order to attain her goal. Your child will show countless examples of such action at this stage; you probably encounter a number of them every day without thinking. If you make a conscious effort to notice your child solving problems in this way, you will be surprised at her ingenuity!

For instance, you may want to repeat the scenario we examined earlier in the book of trying to hand your child a toy horizontally so that it is blocked by the vertical slats of her crib. Eventually, after a chance rotation of the toy, your child will become quite adept at slipping the toy through the slats.

Your child faces a major limitation, however; she is able to experiment successfully only after chance success. In other words, only after she stumbles upon a solution does she become aware of that solution. This stumbling, however, is the final step toward the ability to think out the solution to a sensorimotor problem beforehand. Your child develops that ability in the next stage, the final stage of sensorimotor development.

Bear in mind the emergent nature of Stage V skills: your child's way of problem solving is not an instant reaction, as yours is, but a steadily more proficient series of adaptations. With what kinds of games, toys, and other play can you engage your child to nurture this aspect of her intellect?

Imitation

At this stage your toddler can imitate better than ever before. If you deliberately and slowly touch your forehead as she watches, she will try to touch her own forehead the same way. If you repeat this activity again the next day, you will see her imitate you very efficiently.

Your baby began to imitate your behavior in Stage IV. She was able to approximate behaviors that were not too different from her own spontaneous behavior, but she could rarely do it on her first try. Now, however, she is able to proficiently imitate behavior that is entirely new to her. She doesn't stumble onto the act that she is trying to imitate. Notice that once she learns to imitate an action or a rhyme (or both together), she will want to repeat it over and over again.

To imitate, your baby has to mentally represent another's actions. She must adapt to the situation by changing herself in the face of the present conditions, something far more difficult than simply adding to what she already can do. In imitating a new action, your child must change the structure of what she knows.

Here are some ideas to consider when encouraging your child to imitate:

Pat-a-cake.

Go through the rhyming song with motions and see your child imitate what you say and do. "The Itsy Bitsy Spider" and "Twinkle Twinkle Little Star" are good for this, as well.

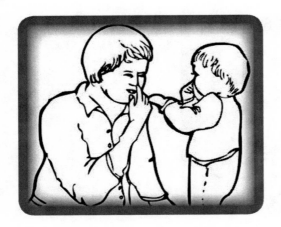

"Here we go round the mulberry bush!"

This song promotes coordination of the spoken word with hand and body gestures. With your child seated in front of you, sing, "This is the way we touch our nose, touch our nose, touch our nose…." Name different parts of your face as you continue. You can create countless variations on this theme ("This is the way we blink our eyes, blink our eyes, blink our eyes…."). Thus you can prompt your child to consciously and deliberately imitate various body movements.

Can your child imitate you wrapping and unwrapping objects or opening and closing zippers?

Encourage rhythm instrument imitations.

You chime a triangle three times; how does your child respond? Sing to her and vary the rhythm of the song; how does she respond?

Household activities.

Does your child try to imitate chores such as dusting, vacuuming, washing dishes, or setting the table?

Cause and Effect, Time, and Space

Suppose you give your child a plastic jar with an interesting toy inside it. She tries unsuccessfully to open the jar. Then she holds out the jar and urges you to open it, but you pay no attention to her. In Stage V, chances are she will take your hand and place the jar in it so that you will open the jar for her.

Your child has now mastered the idea that other people as well as other objects can cause results. She even solicits the help of others in solving problems. She has differentiated the means to an end to such an extent that she now realizes she can use someone else as her means to attain a goal. Now you can also expect your toddler to involve you in her games—to intervene whenever she cannot reach something, for instance. She will gesture and call out to you to retrieve her toy or place it somewhere.

In Stage V, your child sees objects as well as people as potential instruments to an end. How can you get involved? Start by remembering that for the toddler between the ages of twelve and eighteen months, toys take on immense importance. Your toddler is ready and looking for occasions to play. Stage-appropriate toys are enormously valuable now. A few suggestions:

Shape sorters.

Challenge your child to place geometrically shaped objects
into the corresponding holes. This strengthens her idea
of herself as someone who can cause things to happen
Opening and closing the shape sorter to retrieve the shapes
gives an opportunity for trial and error learning as well as
reinforcing the ideas of object permanence, space, time,
and cause and effect.

Peg people or peg animals.

Made from wood or plastic, these toys can be put into and transported in a small pull truck with wheels.

Popper beads.

These large, colorful plastic beads fit into each other and pop out when separated.

Simple puzzles.

Puzzles with a few large pieces help your child learn about spatial relations. The best type for this age group has small knobs on the pieces for your child to lift and hold. Puzzles also improve hand-eye coordination.

A set of wooden blocks.

A set of plastic measur-ing cups for water.

A sandbox.

Graduated colorful plastic rings that can be stacked on a post.

A wooden pounding bench with mallet.

A scooter.

The ones children push with both feet on the floor are best.

A doll carriage.

Between twelve and eighteen months your child will particularly enjoy these types of toys, which provide her opportunities to advance her intellectual skills during playtime. However, you can "manufacture" many other toys at home that will work equally well. For instance:

Attach a piece of rope to a shoebox as a pull truck.

Allow your child to play with dry cereal such as
Cheerios® or Kix® and pots and pans.

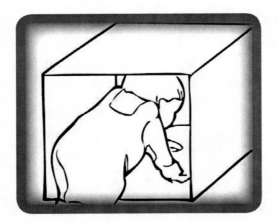

Provide a large cardboard box for your child to crawl into and out of.

Make your own shape sorter.

Cut a circle the size of a ping-pong ball in the plastic top of a coffee can. Provide three small wiffle balls (such as golfers use to practice) and three blocks for your child to use as sorters.

Use plastic cups and other plastic containers at bath time to encourage water pouring.

Encourage stacking.

Stacking toys is an excellent activity. Stack some blocks. If you put a colored block in the middle of a stack of plain-colored blocks, will your child reach for it?

Spatial relations.

Color one side of a cardboard tube. Will your child turn it in order to see the colored side?

Toy tools.

Give your child large plastic nuts and bolts to screw together. She will particularly enjoy these if she likes to imitate grown-up tool use.

Filling containers.

Drop clothespins into transparent plastic bottles; drop toy cars into large envelopes.

Do-it-yourself nesting toys.

For nesting toys, try using paper cups or shoeboxes.

The Object Concept

In Stage V your child's understanding of object permanence becomes increasingly sophisticated. In Stage IV, if you hid an object in one place, then moved it to a second and third hiding place, your baby looked for the object where she found it the last time it was hidden. This meant that she had formed a simple connection between the object and its hiding place. The Stage V child, however, can finally follow a hidden object through a series of hiding places. She knows that the object's previous hiding places don't necessarily matter, because the object may have moved to a different spot. This implies a new and enlarged understanding of the ways objects exist in the world.

This advance in representational thought is in many ways exactly what your child has been working toward for all these months. It signifies a wholly different type of intelligence.

Still, your child has much growing to do. Following a sequence of displacements is impressive, but it is only the threshold of a completely mature understanding of object permanence. As yet, these displacements must be visible in order for your child to follow them. If you place a toy inside a box, for example, then place the box behind a screen and remove the toy from the box, your child will not think to look behind the screen when handed the empty box. It will be another few months before she can do that. Stage VI (between the ages of eighteen months and two years) is the period in which your child fully masters the ability to think about things even when they are not there or when they are moved from place to place. She will have outgrown sensorimotor intelligence and will be able to form mental images of things. Thus she can have an image stand for the real thing.

In Stages III and IV peek-a-boo games were totally appropriate play because your child was in the process of constructing the concept of object permanence. Your child found it remarkable that an object could disappear one moment only to return the next. She thought that a disappearing object had completely vanished. Why and how did it reappear? That puzzle created an intense interest in peek-a-boo games.

In Stage V, your child may lose interest in peek-a-boo games. Seeing an object reappear isn't such a thrill anymore because your child no longer believes that it ceased to exist when she couldn't see it. Now, however, she will begin to show interest in games of hide and seek. Because your child now knows that the object must be around somewhere, the challenge is to find it. (Before Stage V, hide and seek is not much fun, because your child is not yet certain that a hidden object will definitely be found.) Games you can play to enhance this new ability include:

- HIDDEN TOY — Hide a toy, and then join your baby in looking for it.

- CRUMPLING PAPER — The process of crumpling is fascinating for your child to watch; if you then place the ball of paper in a bucket (perhaps also containing a small toy), will she be interested in finding it?

- CONTINUE PLAYING WITH THE JACK-IN-THE-BOX

- "READ" BOOKS TOGETHER — Laminated cardboard pages of rhymes, songs, and simple stories are the best.

- "HIDE" FROM YOUR CHILD — Hide behind a door, leaving your head partially exposed. Encourage your child to find you, and express delight when she succeeds.

- PLAY HIDE AND SEEK — Let your child "hide" and you "try" to find her. Pretend you can't find her initially, then do. Try using a large cardboard box as a hiding place for your child while you go hunting for her.

Language

By her first birthday, it is not unusual for a baby to have a vocabulary of three or four words. She acts in response to speech, comes when called, understands commands, babbles expressively, and looks in specific places when asked where some object or person is. By the time she is two years old, she will have mastered somewhere between two hundred and one thousand words. From this point forward, vocabulary acquisition becomes very rapid indeed!

Here are some suggestions for meaningful interactions:

- Encourage your child to use social words: bye-bye, love you, etc.
- Use action words to describe your child's actions.
- Point to and name objects in your child's immediate en vironment.
- React with enthusiasm to your child's efforts to talk; smile and repeat her words.

Please note while every child develops differently, if your child does not seem to be developing speech by the end of Stage V, it may be an indication of an underlying problem. You should consult your pediatrician regarding your child's progress to rule out any abnormalities.

From Newborn to Toddler

Your child has come a long way. By the time she reaches eighteen months of age, she will be able to walk, talk a little, and efficiently problem-solve through trial and error. She experiments by purposely varying her actions to discover what will happen. She understands that not only she but also other people and objects can cause things to happen. She has constructed an increasingly sophisticated under-standing of the physical world around her, including puzzling out the finer nuances of object permanence.

Your toddler is on her way to moving beyond sensorimo-tor intelligence, which, though it has served her well, is a knowledge system restricted to information she can gather with her five senses. Now that is she beginning to develop a symbolic system, using words to represent the things around her, she is able to represent objects and events mentally, by imaging them. In Stage VI, this will enable her to solve problems without having to engage in physical trial and error. Your child is poised to move beyond her focus on the here and now to become a truly thinking person.

SUMMARY OF INTELLECTUAL ATTAINMENTS — STAGE V: TWELVE TO EIGHTEEN MONTHS

Note: Abilities develop with great variety among Stage V children; month divisions for the achievements at this stage are less useful than in previous stages.

- She is capable of trial and error learning.
- She discovers new sequences of actions in order to solve problems.
- She systematically and intentionally varies her actions to discover how the variations change the outcome.
- She sees objects and people as instrumental to her goals.
- She enjoys discovering spatial relations.
- Her sense of physical causality improves.
- Her object concept improves.
- Her imitation improves.
- She develops early language skills.

stage 6: eighteen to twenty-four months

The keystone of independent, symbolic human thought can be found in two awe-inspiring words: what if...? The incredibly powerful concept behind these words is accountable for the remarkable progress your child makes during this stage.

What if your child could use mental symbols to represent things that are absent from his view? What if he could mentally represent the external world through words, signs, gestures, memory, imagery, and symbols? And what if he could combine these features of mental growth to reach a desired goal?

In Stage VI, your child begins to do all of those things.
You are witnessing the birth of symbolic thought. This new
"what if" development heralds the start of a cognitive revol-
ution that frees your child from the constraints of the here
and now, opening a world of possibilities to him, including
(but by no means limited to), deferred imitation, imagination, and creative "let's pretend" play.

SAFETY CHECK

In Stage VI, all the previous safety warnings of Stage V still
apply. Your child's sense of adventure is much better developed than his judgment. Teach him about possible dangers
and the proper ways to avoid them (such as not touching a
hot stove, looking both ways before crossing a street) but
by no means expect him to be able to handle these types of
situations on his own for a long time. Keep in mind that your
child will be more inclined to imitate your behavior than he
is to listen to your words alone, so the best way to teach him
safe behavior is to model it for him.

Symbolic Thought

The ability to mentally represent the world around him
has dramatic and far-reaching consequences for your child,
and will, by the end of Stage VI, ignite nothing less than an
explosion of mental power. We can now truly say that your

child has the ability to think, not just the ability to produce intelligent actions.

How do you know that your child is capable of mental representation? The Stage VI child can perform two important acts indicating that he has attained the representational system:

1. He can solve problems without engaging in trial and error.
2. He can postpone imitating an observed behavior until a later time.

Problem Solving Through Invention

If your child can solve simple problems without the physical contact and trial and error of Stage V, then he must be figuring things out in his head before applying his conclusions.

Suppose a twenty-one-month-old child sees, for the first time, an interesting marionette resting on top of a bookshelf in his room. A thin, loose string hangs from the figure and dangles just out of reach. The child walks to the bookcase, turns over a nearby milk crate normally used to store toys, stands on it, grabs the string, and pulls the marionette to the floor.

In this example, there is no experimenting at all. The child did not go through a series of failed attempts to get the marionette; he saw the problem, mentally constructed a solution, and then implemented it. His "what if" instinct operated flawlessly.

Physical groping has been replaced by mental groping. Not surprisingly, your child reaches solutions much faster in Stage VI than he did in Stage V.

At this stage of your child's development, your goal should be to provide him with the fullest and richest play opportunities possible. Wherever you can, let your child initiate the activities. Your child will be bored and frustrated with any attempt to impose a rigid teaching agenda on his activities, so relax and let his games be spontaneous, self-chosen, and, above all, fun.

Here are a few suggestions:

Push and pull toys.

These toys provide occasions for problem solving. What happens when an obstacle blocks the toy's path, or an object keeps falling off its resting place as it moves?

Nesting toys.

Use these to encourage your child to figure out spatial relations—what toys go into what, or what must be stacked on what.

Simple puzzles.

These engage your child's ability to reason out what fits where.

Shape sorters.

These help your child activate problem-solving techniques involving geometric forms.

Delayed Imitation

One day, a friend and her three-year-old come to visit you and your child. Noticing how much attention your child receives, the three-year-old decides to pound a toy on the high-chair tray. A few days later, your child, alone with you, decides to pound away on his own high chair with the same toy in his hand! The other child is not present; somehow your child stored the event and now decides to retrieve it.

Deferred imitation is convincing evidence of your child's ability to symbolize things: to store an act, a phrase, or a game in memory and, at an appropriate later time, to retrieve it and act it out.

Here are a few enriching imitation activities that your child will enjoy in Stage VI.

Dancing provides musical fun and increases your child's awareness of his body.

Dress-up.

Wearing adult clothes to "try on" different social roles encourages your child to accommodate himself to various forms of social behavior.

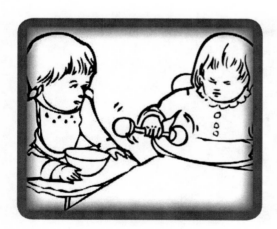

Toy telephones.

These toys—and later on, real phones—encourage verbal exchange and imitation of adults or siblings.

"Painting."

Give your child a paintbrush and a bucket of water and encourage him to "help" you complete a painting job.

Encourage your child to imitate and help out in the garden.

Sound imitation.

Imitate the sounds animals and objects make, such as birds, cats, trucks, and trains. Encourage your child to make the sounds, too.

Pretend Games

Encourage your child to act out someone else's feelings and actions. Pretending that he is asleep or sneezing and coughing is more than mere fun—it means he is accommodating himself to a different situation. Playing with dolls and puppets represents the same type of action. Dancing provides musical fun and increases your child's awareness of his body.

Stage VI Knowledge: Time, Space, Causality, and the Object Concept

Your child throws a ball under a sofa. Without hesitation, he sets out to look for it behind the sofa. This incident illustrates his maturing conceptual development, demonstrating his ability to mentally represent things and their displacements in space. Not only does he realize that the ball has a permanence of its own, but he can imagine the invisible displacements taking place as the ball travels under the sofa and comes to rest behind it.

In addition to showing a mature object concept, this example typifies your child's ability in Stage VI to combine concepts of time, space, causality, and object permanence to yield an expectation of where the ball should be.

Your child demonstrates his understanding of space and spatial relations in many different ways every day. He opens a gate to get through a fence, or, when you and he return home from the grocery store, he points in recognition to his house as you drive toward it.

Of course, we can't expect a completely mature understanding of time, space, causality, or object permanence at two years of age. The understanding of these concepts develops continually. Physics, the formal study of these concepts, extends them to their theoretical limits. So it is fair to say that while your child in this stage is not an accomplished physicist, he is a budding one!

Keep in mind that although your child's ideas about the physical world may seem strange to you at times, from his perspective they make sense. He may blink to turn the lights on, bang his foot on the floor to make the window open wider, and move his own hand to make you move yours. His view of the world is egocentric, and while he does understand that other people and objects cause things to happen, he may mistakenly believe that his own actions have caused a particular unrelated outcome.

Most of what you did with your child in Stage V will be equally interesting and enjoyable in Stage VI. You may also want to introduce some new toys and games that are both appropriate and exciting in this, the final stage of the sensorimotor period. Here are a few examples.

More baby books.

Picture books are wonderful for this age; they help teach language skills. When using animal picture books, make the sounds that the animals make. Stress colors, shapes, and sounds when reading through the books with your child.

Finger paints.

Wind-up toys.

Your child shows his understanding of cause and effect when he looks for an explanation as to why a wind-up toy continues its action.

Play dough.

Puppet show.

With your hands hidden from your child's sight behind a pillow, move a puppet back and forth. Your child's first reaction is to look at you in awe. Have you anything at all to do with the event?

Sand and water play.

Learning parts of the body.

Point out your child's ears, eyes, nose, and so on, talking about what each part is for. ("Your eyes are to see with.") Cover your child's eyes, then mouth, etc. Then cover your own. Keep taking turns. This helps your child begin to identify body parts and realize that each one has a certain function.

Filling and emptying.

Allow your child to fill plastic milk bottles with sand, water, or Cheerios®, and then empty them.

Use squeeze bottles in the bathtub to encourage experimentation.

Purchase or make a "do-it-myself board" with hinges, knobs, locks, etc.

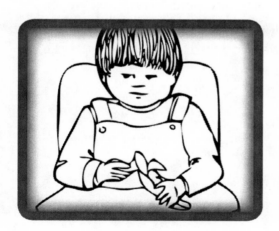

Banana peel.

To encourage detailed finger movements, let your child help you in the kitchen by giving him a banana to peel.

Also—try games and a puzzle or two:

Matching blocks.

When playing with blocks, pick one up and show it to
your child. Ask him to hand you a block "just like" the one
you are holding. Use color, size, and texture. However,
remember to ask your child to match only one feature at a
time. For example, "Can you find a blue block just like
this one?"

Play ball.

Sit on the floor with your child with both of your legs apart and your feet touching. Roll a ball between you.

Peg puzzles.

Use simple, store-bought peg puzzles. Your child is ready for puzzles with five to seven pieces.

Blocks, blocks, blocks.

Provide more complex block sets with several varying shapes and sizes. Allow your child to play freely with these.

Push/pull and carry games are wonderful for this stage.

Let's pretend.

At the age of two, most children are ready for make-believe games. Encourage them!

Provide your child with paper and crayons for scribbling.

Roughhousing.

Your child will enjoy gentle roughhousing at this stage (tickling and "wrestling," for example). Remember to keep your play easygoing; your child may still be easily overwhelmed.

Art project.

Help your child make a collage out of everyday materials such as paper, yarn, and fabric scraps.

Clothing fasteners.

Give your child a cloth toy with lots of different closings:
hooks, buttons, zippers, flaps, and pockets.

Where did it go?

At this age your child will like toys with hidden parts that
disappear when knobs are turned, etc.

Pushing buttons.

Your child likes to play with knobs, keys, and buttons, so toy cash registers, telephones, and similar toys will be a big hit at this age.

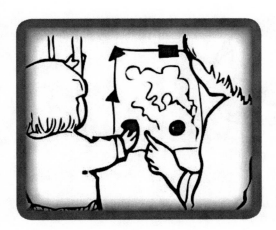

Play games with magnets on the refrigerator.

"Telling" time.

Use time concepts when you speak to your child: "Today we will visit Grandma. Tomorrow we will go to the zoo. Yesterday we planted flowers. Now we are going to eat lunch."

Practice stringing large beads of different shapes (spheres, cubes, etc.).

Magnifying glass.

Let your child experiment with a non-breakable magnifying glass. He will discover that when he looks at objects through the glass, they look bigger than they did before.

Give your child more complicated nesting toys.

Paper games.

Hold up a large piece of newsprint and encourage your child to punch a hole through the paper. As he does this, he not only discovers the properties of the paper itself, he also invents things he can do to the paper (such as tearing or poking holes in it). Try crumpling the paper and playing with the crumpled balls.

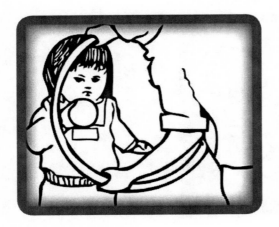

Target practice.

Help your child to throw a ball through a hula hoop. Also give your child lots of balls (of varying sizes and textures) to practice hitting, throwing, and rolling.

Allow your child to climb in and out of spaces.

Clothespins.

Drop colored clothespins into an open coffee can.
Then attach the clothespins to the outside of the can.

All of these suggestions (and any variations you might think of) promote the development of your child's construction of the concepts of time, space, causality, and object permanence.

The End of the Beginning

Your child has arrived at the final stage of sensorimotor intelligence, a stage that designates the end of his reliance on the here and now. Concrete, empirical experience is no longer your child's primary basis of knowing. The process of cognitive development has brought him to a point where he can represent objects with signs or symbols. What an accomplishment!

This new development is the start of the ability to think. As we have seen, your child can now solve problems without actually engaging in trial and error, that is, without direct, physical groping. Also, he can postpone imitating an observed behavior until a later time. By Stage VI, your child is already well furnished with a multitude of schemes; all he needs is to evoke these schemes mentally. The implications of this are far-reaching.

Your child's concept of object permanence, space, time, and causality are integrated at a level that enables him to construct his own reality of the world around him. Not only does he now realize that each object has a permanence of its own, he can also imagine the invisible displacements that occur when an object is hidden.

Your child is no longer passive, dependent, and reactive, as he was at birth, a mere two years ago. He is now a thinking person who knows he exists as one of the many entrancing elements of the world. Vast horizons of growth await your child, but he will approach them now equipped with his own unique ideas, reflections, and goals.

SUMMARY OF INTELLECTUAL ATTAINMENTS — STAGE VI: EIGHTEEN TO TWENTY-FOUR MONTHS

As in Stage V, these milestones are not broken down by month, because each child develops differently. However, every child will show all these attainments by the end of this stage.

- He invents solutions before acting to solve a problem.
- He can defer imitation of an observed action until a later time.
- He follows displacement of objects as they are moved from place to place.
- He seeks physical explanations for events.

Bibliography

Barnett, W. Steven. "Long-Term Cognitive and Academic Effects of Early Childhood Education on Children in Poverty." Preventive Medicine 27 (1998): 204-207.

Braga, Joseph D. and Laurie L. Braga. Child Development and Early Childhood Education. Chicago: Model Cities-Chicago Committee on Urban Opportunity, 1973.

Bruner, J. Acts of Meaning. Cambridge, MA: Harvard University Press, 1990.

—. The Culture of Education. Cambridge, MA: Harvard University Press, 1996.

Cataldo, Christine. Infant and Toddler Programs: A Guide to Very Early Education. Reading, MA: Addison-Wesley, 1983.

Clarke, Jeffrey M. "Neuroanatomy, Brain Structure and Function." In Neuropsychology: A Handbook of Perception and Cognition, 2nd ed., edited by Dahlia W. Zaidel, 29-52. San Diego: Academic Press, 1994.

Conel, J. L. The Postnatal Development of the Human Cerebral Cortex. Cambridge, MA: Harvard University Press, 1959.

Einon, Dorothy. Play With a Purpose. New York: Simon & Schuster, 1983.

Goodson, Barbara D., Jean I. Layzer, Robert G. St. Pierre, Lawrence S. Bernstein, and Michael Lopez. "Effectiveness of a Comprehensive, Five-Year Family Support Program for Low-Income Children and their Families: Findings from the Comprehensive Child Development Program." Early Childhood Research Quarterly 15, no.1 (2000): 5-39.

Gopnik, Alison, Andrew N. Meltzoff, and Patricia K. Kuhl. The Scientist in the Crib: Minds, Brains, and How Children Learn. New York: William Morrow and Company, 1999.

Gordon, Ira. Baby Learning Through Baby Play: A Parent's Guide for the First Two Years of Life. New York: St. Martin's Press, 1970.

Grasselli, Rose N., and Priscilla A. Hegner. Playful Parenting: Games to Help Your Infants and Toddlers Grow Physically, Mentally, and Emotionally. New York: Richard Marek Publishers, 1981.

Guralnick, Michael J. "Effectiveness of Early Intervention for Vulnerable Children: A Developmental Perspective." American Journal on Mental Retardation 102, no. 4 (1998): 319–345.

Haberland, Karl. Cognitive Psychology, 2nd ed. Boston: Allyn and Bacon, 1997.

Hubel, D. H., and T. N. Wiesel. "Receptive fields of cells in striate cortex of very young, visually inexperienced kittens." Journal of Neurophysiology 26 (1963): 994-1002.

Jacob, S.H. Foundations for Piagetan Education. Lanham, MD: University Press of America, 1984.

—. Your Baby's Mind: How to Make the Most of the Critical First Two Years. Holbrook, MA: Bob Adams, Inc., 1992.

Lehane, Stephen. Help Your Baby Learn: 100 Piaget-Based Activities for the First Two Years of Life. Englewood Cliffs, NJ: Prentice-Hall, 1976.

Liebert, Robert M., Rita Wicks-Nelson, and Robert Kail. Developmental Psychology. Englewood Cliffs, NJ: Prentice-Hall, 1984.

Maynard, Fredelle Bruser. The Child Care Crisis. New York: Simon & Schuster, 1985.

McCall, Robert B. Infants. Cambridge, MA: Harvard University Press, 1979.

Nash, Madeline, J. "Fertile Minds." Time Magazine, February 1997, 51.

Newson, John, and Elizabeth Newson. Toys and Playthings. London: George Allen & Unwin, 1979.

Piaget, Jean. The Origins of Intelligence in Children. New York: International Universities Press, 1952.

—. The Psychology of Intelligence. Totowa, N.J.: Littlefield, Adams, & Co., 1972a.

—. Science of Education and the Psychology of the Child. New York: The Viking Press, 1972b.

Restak, Richard M. The Brain: The Last Frontier. New York: Warner Books, 1979.

Saunders, Ruth, and Ann M. Bingham-Newman. Piagetan Perspective for Preschools: A Thinking Book for Teachers. Englewood Cliffs, NJ: Prentice-Hall, 1984.

Scheibel, A. B. "Dentritic correlates of higher cognitive function." In Neurobiology of Higher Cognitive Function, edited by A. B. Scheibel and A. F. Wechsler, 239-270. New York: Guilford Press, 1990.

Shaw, Benjamin, et al. "Emotional Support From Parents Early in Life, Aging, and Health." Psychology and Aging 19, no. 1 (March 2004).

Smolak, Linda. Infancy. Englewood Cliffs, NJ: Prentice-Hall, 1986.

Sroufe, L. Alan. Child Development: Its Nature and Course. New York: Alfred A. Knopf, 1988.

Zitman, Susan. All Day Care. New York: Random House, 1990.